ÅKE WIBERG

Swedish Entrepreneur & Politician

shortened, English edition for family

Mats Larsson

plus family tree &oral histories
of the *Bahamas Wibergs*

Edited by Eric Wiberg

The original Swedish publication has been financed by the Åke Wiberg Foundation and published together with the Foundation for Economic and Corporate Historical Research (EHFF) Uppsala, 2007.
This edition published by Island Books, New York, 2018.

*dedicated to all descendants
and relatives of Åke Wiberg*

published by Island Books
New York, NY, USA
eric@ericwiberg.com

Copyright © Mats Larsson, author – Part II
Copyright © Eric Wiberg, editor – Parts I & III

ISBN: 978-0-9994378-2-7, 999437828
Library of Congress PCN: 2017962597

Designed and printed by Onomatopo, India

This edition 2018

NOT FOR SALE

It is a special limited edition compiled by members of Åke Wiberg's family and is intended only for members of his family. It has been made possible by the gracious permission of many organizations, including the author, the publishers, and the Åke Wiberg Foundation, on the understanding that its contents were exclusively for private use.

TABLE OF CONTENTS

PART I

Author and Contributors / page 1
Introduction, by Atlantis Books / 3
Introduction, Key Dates, by Eric Wiberg / 5
Family Tree Photos from Ancestry Book *Bjära Släkten*/ 13
Family Tree Photos and Short Biographies / 19

PART II

Preface, by Mats Larsson / 39
The Foundation – Instrument or Monument? by Göran Mörner / 41
Childhood and Youth / 49
The School Years / 59
At the University of Lund / 65
Family and National Politics / 67
Culture, Politics, and Contacts / 75
The Åke Wiberg Foundation / 77
A Long, Drawn Out Illness / 81
Active to the Very End / 89
Legacy / 95
Photos and Captions / 97

PART III

Interview with Dr. Märta Holmström by Eric Wiberg, 1992 /101
Interview with Gunnel Lindroth by Eric Wiberg, 2011 / 107
Interview with Dr. Holmström by Jane Wiberg, 1999 / 117

    Part I: Family, Childhood, Early Life / 119
    Part II: *Examen*, Lund, Medical School / 125
    Part III: Apertin, Caught in Norway in WWII, Nazi Soldiers, Later Life / 129

Farmor – Personal Reminisces and Anecdotes / 151
Bahamas Wibergs' Marriage Matrix / 155

PART I

AUTHOR AND CONTRIBUTORS

Author MATS LARSSON is Professor of Economic History at Uppsala University and manages the Uppsala Center for Business History. He specializes in research concerning business and finance history, and is the author of two books about The Bonnier Corporation.

Benefactor the ÅKE WIBERG FOUNDATION was created in 1954, and has since then provided resources for scientific research, primarily in medicine and the humanities. The Foundation has also supported children's causes and youth care activities, as well as teaching and educational matters. The Åke Wiberg Foundation is amongst Sweden's twenty largest research-oriented foundations.

Original publisher ATLANTIS, Stockholm, provided support and introductions. Atlantisbok.se

Translator ROGER HINCHLIFFE has been popularizing leading Swedish writers and composers for over 25 years. His recordings of his English translations of timeless classic Swedish songs are regularly heard on Swedish radio. We are happy to include here his award-winning CD *Swedes on Love* as a special present to Åke

Wiberg's family. Please visit **amanofhiswords.com** for more. Roger was a Peace Corps volunteer who left Cornell for Colombia (the country), then worked his way across the Atlantic on a banana boat with his Swedish wife to live in Sweden for decades.

Interviewees DR. MÄRTA (HOLMSTRÖM) WIBERG and GUNNEL (WIBERG) LINDROTH graciously provided their time and energy to recording their life's details and adventures.

Interviewers JANE McDERMID WIBERG, Åke's daughter-in-law, ERIC WIBERG, grandson.

Cover designer SANCHIT GOEL of Delhi, India, has worked on two dozen projects with Eric.

Publisher, editor ERIC WIBERG, grandson, is the overall organizer of this project. He takes full responsibility for errors, omissions, mistakes, exclusions, and mistranslations. Ericwiberg.com

Note: *If every Swedish word was italicized, the text would be awkward, so they have not been.*

INTRODUCTION
(By publisher, Atlantis Books)

Today Åke Wiberg is a relatively anonymous person. He was, in any case, an important political and business figure in the Malmö region from the early 1930's through the early 1960's. As the owner of the Malmö Stocking Factory, he managed one of the area's largest textile manufacturers, and through his political engagement he helped rid the Swedish Conservative Party of its Nazi sympathizers.

Politics took him to the Swedish Parliament in the 1940's, but illness forced him to retire from politics after ten years of service. He energetically devoted his last dozen years to a number of cultural projects, including work for the National Arts Council and the East Asian Museum. Åke Wiberg was a man whose determination and personality have apparently moved many of those who knew him

INTRODUCTION
(By grandson, Eric Wiberg)

The genesis of this project was when I was given a wonderful book about my grandfather that I could not read. As I approach age fifty, rather than wait till I am fluent in Swedish, I decided to invest in translating relevant parts of it into English. The goal of this book is not simply to tell Åke Wiberg's life, but to just to describe he and his first wife as living, vibrant people. One very specific goal is to explain why nine direct descendants over three generations live in the Bahamas, whereas only five live in Sweden. Why are there any what I call *Bahamas Wibergs* at all? In 2018, Åke Wiberg has eleven great-grandchildren: two in California (Norwegian speakers), five in the Bahamas (one Finnish, two Swedish speakers), one in Connecticut, and three in Sweden. It is possible others reside in Switzerland.

Since less than a quarter of that generation grew up in Sweden, the odds are that his family will grow further and further away from that base. Although all have Swedish passports, only two were born in the country. His only daughter and granddaughter live in Sweden, as do three great-grandsons. The rest have become *utländska Svenskar*, or *Svenskariutlandet*: a badge of pride meaning *overseas Swedes*, or *Swedes out of the land*, – far away. His son became the longest serving Swedish Consul-General, and his grandson and his wife serve in that capacity, as does a grandson-in-law. Each generation after him has another lawyer in it. But his legacy in real estate in Sweden is hardly even a shadow of its former self, though some of the art remains.

This poses interesting challenges for preserving his legacy. Most of a generation has been supported in some form or another educationally by his legacy. It is therefore incumbent on us, his English-speaking relatives, to preserve, interpret, and spread the story of this amazing man. With support from a close-knit family and a strong code of values, extremely hard work and dedication, he built a future not just for himself, but for his family, his employees, and his colleagues. For a number of reasons, perhaps some of them political, his many contributions to Swedish economics and politics as well as architecture and art, have gone underappreciated.

Åke Wiberg (who is referred to herein by both of his names, perhaps out of a sign of respect), created an amazing legacy, but did stay healthy enough to defend it into old age. His company dominated an impressive market, including northern Germany, Benelux, and all of Scandinavia. Some machines had 30,000 moving parts, and were always replaced by the latest model. Although he was controversial, my sense is that Åke Wiberg was respected and admired by many. Though he may have led an imperfect personal life (who hasn't?), he also suffered physically, and died tragically. Through his accomplishments, he left behind a generous legacy, not just for we, his direct descendants, but for innumerable beneficiaries of his foundation.

This is meant to be enjoyable reading. The translator, Roger Hinchliffe, and I selected passages which tell the human-interest story, as it relates to his family.

The grainy details of the business empire and ascent in politics are basically passed over to cover his family life, country and city homes, and legacy. I have taken the liberty of adding two interviews of our beloved Farmor, Åke's first wife, as well as Gunnel Lindroth, who relates how she and her husband Arne first settled in Bahamas, then welcomed Farmor's son Anders. The purpose of this book is to inform, enlighten, entertain, and give all of us stories to tell our grandchildren. Please play it forward.

Key Dates in Bahamas, *Bahamas Wiberg* Anecdotes:

The Bahamas were first inhabited around 1000 A.D. by Lucayans of the Taino tribe who named it *ba ha ma* for "big upper middle land." Soon after he arrived in 1492 Columbus and his brother Bartholomew were granted personal ownership of the islands, meaning that there are no records of the ensuing genocide. By 1513, Ponce de Leon found the 700 or so larger islands empty of people.

Presently there are roughly 400,000 inhabitants, of whom roughly 90% are of African and 5% of European descent.

In 1648British dissenters from Bermuda settled Eleuthera tenuously, in 1670 the British king granted lands there to investors, and in 1718 it became a colony. Theabolishment of British slavery 1807-1834 increased the population of freed slaves. HRH the Duke of Windsor and Wallis Simpson lived in Nassau during WWII – he as governor – which encouraged tourism.

The 'father of tourism' was Sir Stafford Sands of the UBP, or United Bahamian Party, a legal oligarchy of wealthy merchants in Nassau. In 1952 when the Lindroths arrived a semi-autonomous Legislative Council ruled. Then in 1964 Sir Roland Symonette became the first Premier. Ann was born in New York City, where Mom and Dad owned an apartment high up at #340 Easts 64thStreet, between 1st and 2nd Avenues, as they "kept a toothbrush in both places," and doing so would ensure the children would retain US citizenship.

The political situation was in turmoil – in 1967 Sir Lynden Pindling was elected the first majority-rule Premier, and the following year, when John was born in the US, he became Prime Minister (he lived literally down the road; Mom and Dad were neighbor to finance ministers and senators). Dad tells that Pindling was to give a keynote address to the United Nations in New York and was on the same plane as Mom, Dad and young Ann. Due to weather, the plane was placed in a holding pattern and it was clear the prime minister would miss his speech. Then Ann, whilst running in the aisles, hit her head and bled. This soon became a sufficient "situation" to merit emergency clearance to land, and Pindling made it to the UN!

Eric was born before independence, and James less than a year before that day on July 10, 1973. This means that the first two generations of *Bahamas Wibergs* lived in a British colony – the TV programs from London insisted that the UK was the world superpower (they were not). One effect of independence was "white flight" (Sands emigrated to Spain with his fortune in 1967 and others went to the UK, Australia, South Africa, South Carolina). Another was a "correction" whereby the new government booted out expatriates to make way for nationalizing jobs for locals. The way this was most often achieved to mute the political reaction was simply to cancel work visas on a rolling basis for different individuals. Even the Lindroth children found themselves leaving for Canada and beyond. Many of my childhood classmates left the country, some of them to return, most did not. This has of course stabilized, however Ann left for boarding school in about 1981, John followed by 1982, and Eric by 1983. Of the four of us, John returned full time around 1994 to work at the Manor, and James repatriated to Nassau about 1996. The issues of Bahamian permits and visas – to work, to reside, to become a citizen – have plagued the first two generations, but appear largely to be worked out for the third. Being a family of diplomats and not getting involved in "greasing the wheels" meant going it alone.

Mom and Dad lived at the Manor (in what is now the tool shed) from about 1965-1966, then rented a cottage on adjacent Hibiscus Lane (one over from Sandals, leading to a small cove). With two children, by c.1970 they purchased *Palmeiras* overlooking a pond and the Hobby Horse Racetrack to what was then the Emerald Beach Hotel. They immediately added a tennis court to the north (Dad told me it "saved the marriage!"), and Mom has since perfected the gardens. The back porches, washing area, and large kitchen were added in the 1990s.

Some perspectives: Nurse Ulla of Germany was live-in nanny from 1966 until about 1975. She has two lovely Bahamian daughters. She (and later others) lived in what is now the TV room, which had a flat roof from which you could spectated tennis matches. An elderly Bahamian woman named Gertrude literally came with the house as gardener. She wore a grey uniform, straw hat, and smoked. Later I visited her home with mom to give food.

We once returned from Sweden to a note which read "cat dead." Pets included snakes, turtles, a golden lab named Honey, a black lab or potcake (mutt) named Chippy, birds, numerous other dogs, a few cats, and ducks. Inez, an elderly housekeeper from Arthur's Town Cat Island, sang and carried a water bucket on her head while working. Mom and Dad threw out the television around 1975, replacing doorways with bookshelves.

One of the characteristics of being diplomats in a tropical setting is that entertainment is a way of life (particularly if you also operate a hotel year-round!). Mom and Dad have graciously hosted hundreds of events – highlights have included two Christmas parties attended by Lady Thatcher, events where the bridge Dad built over the paisley-shaped pool collapsed, a 1950s-themed event, tea parties, luncheons, and commemorative dinners.

Dad brought his own Tempura skills from Japan in the 1970s, as well as sausages from Germany and his own pâtés. We've had all manner of musicians (Dad offered to buy us all tutorials in break-dancing), conch fritters, and Swedish delicacies. When I need work in the shipping industry, Mom once reminded a ship owner that his daughter had met her husband at one of our parties!

Our neighbors have had stories to tell as well – the Rounces, the Zilstras, Thompsons, Jim and Mary from the US Embassy, a British WWII vet who used to show us the bullet hole in his tummy. The Rosses were from New Zealand, Mrs. Allen from New York, Senator Moss from Acklins (his wife is a seamstress: I once told Senator Basil Kelly, his rival, that Mr. Moss was losing his mind. Kelly said, "Oh, that's quite already, he never had one!").

It has been popular for Swedish Ambassadors based in Ottawa to visit Nassau on official business in the dead of winter. Dad hosted Olaf Palme in Nassau, and Farmor was his physician. On Harbor Island, Dad is known as "the man who goes to sea and does not come back." Several times he showed up at the Government Dock requesting to be taken out to sea, with no further explanation. Once at sea, a Swedish tall ship (*Falken*) would show up, cannons would go off, he would be saluted aboard, and sail off.... Dad once got Eric and John aboard other tall ships.

FAMILY TREE PHOTOS FROM ÅKE WIBERG'S ANCESTRY BOOK *BJÄRASLÄKTEN*

Yngve is Åke's father. For most readers, he is your great-great-grandfather. With the help of your great-great-grandmother, his wife Thyra (right), they worked extremely hard, took many risks, and made very good business decisions, such as not to supply the German army with shoes in World War I. The intelligent balance of risk and caution enabled them to put Åke and his brothers (including Magnus) to the best schools. That started them off with a very big advantage, if they used the opportunities well, which they did. They were from an area near Gothenburg, on the west coast of Sweden, which faces the North Sea rather than the Baltic Sea, which the capital, Stockholm faces.

Gothenburg has always been the commercial gateway to Sweden, where not only the world's goods, but also ideas arrive along with bananas, coffee and thousands of other items. It was also well stout Swedish ships entered the world's trade. In fact, during the 1930's, one of the port's shipyards, named Götaverken manufactured more ships (by launched gross tonnes) than any other shipyard in the entire world! As for how the name of the city is pronounced, in Swedish it is spelled Göteborg, and pronounced like "yachte-borg," and in English it is usually pronounced "Gothen-burg," but some even say "goat-borg"! (In the 1990s Eric operated tanker ships from Singapore that were built in Gothenburg in the 1970s, and they were very strong – in a way the last of their kind).

ÅKE WIBERG   MÄRTA WIBERG

This is Åke and his wife since the time the met at Lund University, Dr. Märta Holmström Wiberg. For most readers, Åke is your great-grandfather, and Dr. Holmström your great-grandmother on the Swedish/Wiberg side. They lived several places in Sweden together – Lund,

Malmö, Stockholm, Gothenburg and several lovely country homes as well. They even lived in California for a while after the war. Unfortunately, they did not stay married.

Farmor, as she is known to Ann, John, Eric and James, as well as to Grandmommy, used to spend several months a year at *Palmeiras* in Bahamas, and at least one of the Bahamas Wibergs would spend time in Sweden each summer. We were all quite close, and she told some wonderful stories. She had a good sense of humor.

ANDERS WIBERG

,

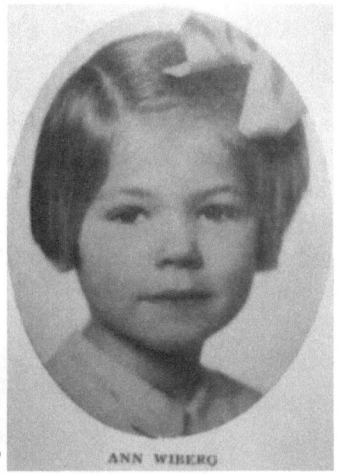
ANN WIBERG

As you can see, Åke and Märta had three children. The oldest is named Sten Anders, but is known by Anders, or Morfar, Papa, or Granddaddy. His picture is above, to the left. He also lived many places, including Sweden, Brazil, the United States, and Bahamas, where he has been living since the mid-1960s. Ask about how many languages he has spoken – there are many!

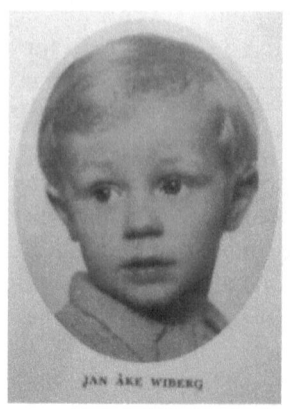

JAN ÅKE WIBERG

The author Mats Larsson spoke with Anders many times about his father Åke. His sister is named Ann, or "Aunt Ann," so she is not confused with her younger niece, Ann (Wiberg) Wachtmeister, who grew up in Bahamas. Aunt Ann lives in Stockholm. She does not have a husband or children. She and her mother used to go to the opera there together.

This is Jan Åke Wiberg. He is named for his father. Most of his adult life he has lived in Switzerland. At one point he wrote history about the French military (like Felix does!). He married a woman from Switzerland, and they had a daughter. He sometimes goes to Sweden, and has also traveled to the Bahamas and throughout Europe.

GUNNEL HELGOSDOTTER WIBERG

This is Gunnel Wiberg. She later married a fellow Swede named Arne Lindroth. They lived a life of adventure and began working for an important Swedish businessman named Axel Wenner-

Gren, who owned Electrolux. In 1952 they moved to the Bahamas to oversee his many business and construction, banking and other interests and investments there. That inspired Anders, whilst on a visit to family business in Colombia, to visit them in Nassau, in 1959, when he was about twenty-four years old.

It was an influential visit, as years later (in 1965) after living in Sweden, New York, Sao Paolo and even a little time in Portugal, he chose those lovely islands to invest in a hotel (yes – Cable Beach Manor!). He settled down with Grandmommy, Mormor, or Jane, where they raised four children – one of them is probably your parent!

Keep reading to hear the story of how Gunnel arrived in the Bahamas. She and Arne had four children (including Ulf and Lizzie), and two of them have spent a lot of time in the Bahamas later in life – Magnus and especially Orjan. Now John Wiberg (to some of you Daddy, Uncle, Godfather, Son or Brother!), has worked closely with Orjan for many years, and Sofia works closely with his wife (Aunt) Amanda Lindroth…. It truly is a small world…… ..

FAMILY TREE PHOTOS AND SHORT BIOGRAPHIES

This is Ralph Manewal McDermid, Jane (Grandmommy's) father. A branch of his family were captains and lawyers from Scotland named Fairbanks who settled in about 1649 in Dedham, Massachusetts. The house is now a museum, and the oldest of its kind in America. Fairbanks became a Vice President to Teddy Roosevelt, governor of New Hampshire, and had the Alaskan city named for them. Other relatives moved to the Chicago area and married German-Americans who baked cracker and cookies for American Biscuit Company that became Nabisco. Helped establish the Chicago Wheat and Grain Exchange. Granddad went to law school at Harvard and Grandmommy typed his papers for him whilst raising their first of four children. Jane (b.1939) is their only daughter, and the only one to move overseas. Our family are descended from the large Campbell Clan of Scotland.

Alice M. Connell Dillon McDermid was a classic beauty, and a strong woman. They met at the Republican National Convention in Chicago, waiting for an elevator. Grand-mommy was very short, and Granddaddy, or "Mac," was very tall. She embraced the Episcopal, or Protestant faith, since being an Irish, or Roman Catholic, was  hardly even accepted in America at the time. The couple moved from outside Chicago (the Evanston area) to Boston, then Scarsdale, New York, where Granddad was managing partner of Reid & Priest, a major utility law firm.

They settled in Winter Park, Florida, where their son, daughter, and two grandsons all either graduated or went to summer camp. Grandmommy volunteered at church and a museum for Louis Comfort Tiffany's art. Granddaddy liked to pretend to shoot squirrels, he wrote and told wonderful stories and poems. He loved to fish and had classic cars. He lived from 1905 to 1991, and she from 1906 to 1993. Her last words to me in 1993 were "you are going to become a lawyer!" Of course, she was right, but I didn't know it. Better yet she also predicted, correctly, that I would go to a Catholic university!

Jane Wiberg, born Jane Dillon McDermid outside New York City in 1939. Known to Grandmommy to many, Farmor to some, daughter to two, and Mommy or Sis to others, she has been den mother and more to three brothers, as well as four children and now nearly a dozen grandchildren! Farmor (her mother in law) said what an amazing daughter inlaw she was. Every year Farmor would live with us in Nassau. Even though Mom has been a champion tennis player her whole adult life, and Farmor smoked basically at all times, indoors and out, at the dinner table and in bed, Mom never complained!

Before meeting Dad in the Bahamas in 1964, Mom worked at the *New Yorker Magazine* in New York City, near where she grew up in Scarsdale. After attending Dana Hall School and Briarcliff College, she studied art history at the University of Michigan in Ann Arbor. Now she has one of the finest collections of art, Bahamian and otherwise, in the Bahamas.

Recently, Mom was inducted into the National Tennis Hall of Fame for the Bahamas. That's because she has won just about any tennis tournament that she entered, if not the first year, then the next, whether playing for a country or a country club. For years she played in the CARIFTA tennis matches around the Caribbean. She has been to most of the Caribbean Islands.

Mom was always at Dad's elbow for the weekly rum punch parties at the Manor. Because of custom at the time, she would not initially work at the Manor. However about 1995 she became overall manager and has worked extremely hard to save and turn around that and the Manor. It has never been an easy job, but she also nurtured various artists and even an artistic colony at the Manor for a time. All the while she taught tennis, stayed on top of all four children's educaction, travels, and then growing families.

As the wife of one of the senior-most diplomats in the country, and hostess and then manager of the Manor, Mom has proven to be an extraordinarily accomplished organizer. She is capable of making events from ladies lunches with Irish percelein to costumed Christmas parties for Lady Thatcher seem effortless. She has seen large properties carefully manicured, smote down by hurricanes, and rebuilt, yet she smiles and makes it look easy. One of her secrets is "the closet" in which are kept a Band-Aid and a gift for every person on every occasion. A testament to Mom's loyalty are her many close friends who take turns staying with her in Nassau.

This is Dad, Sten Anders Wiberg, born 1935. When he was a little boy a woman in the same building lost her husband, also named Sten. So Dad's family started calling him by his middle name – Anders – instead, so as not to upset her. Did you know he specialized in publishing law and was student union president with the best roomon campus? That he ran both Bahamas and Caribbean hotel associations? That when he bought the Manor he refused to "bow down" to the local kingpin, and that made him more popular among the black majority who soon took power? He once attended an event hosted by the notorious Baby Doc of Haiti.

Dad has run many charitable groups, including Rotary West Nassau, Skal Club, as well as Consular Corps. When he took long trips for work in the 1970s and 80s, he would hire security guards to protect the family. When the same guards stole our car, Dad reversed the writing on the gear shift, so that he would return to find the car at the bottom of our driveway. He is always ready with a witty story and a hearty laugh. And he has been an avid reader forever.

Generation two of the *Bahamas Wibergs*. Taken at *Palmeiras* around 1987. Eric, James, Ann, John. All attended Lyford Cay School, then St. Andrews, in the Bahamas. Ann went to Madeira first, followed by John to Rectory, then Foreman. Eric followed to Eaglebrook, then St. George's, with James attending Cardigan Mountain, Tabor, and then Hebron Academy. Each studied in Europe for a year: Ann and James in London (then James in

Santander, Spain for a summer), John in Switzerland, and Eric at Oxford, then Lisbon. These four and their eleven children between them have passports to Sweden, the US, UK, Ireland, Finland, and Bahamas.

This is Mom and Dad on their honeymoon to Treasure Cay, Abaco, in the spring of 1966. The stories of how they met and how they engaged, and their honeymoon are so extraordinary that they bear repeating. Mom took a flight to Nassau with a good friend as the first break from their jobs in New York City. Their arrival was photographed, and their names and hotel published in the papers! They stayed at the British Colonial, but when her friend's parents had an accident and she left, Mom remained a few days. She shared a cab to the aiport with some Swedish hydro-engineers. The flight from Newark was grounded by birds. It was Swedish Christmas, and they went together to Ronnie and Joan Carroll's place at Cable Beach, where Mom met Dad, literally across a crowded, smoke-filled room.

The next day he flew to Brazil, she to New York. A year or so later she was visiting Dad at the Manor. He was preoccupied with work, she went to dinner with the son of a South African tennis partner. Dad proposed the next day. They were married at Grace Episcopal Church in Scarsdale. On the flight to honeymoon on Treasure Cay, one of the British flight attendants recognized Dad from when he was in a "brat pack" at the Park Manor Hotel, Market Street, Nassau (it still stands. The pack included Dr. Bev Bowen and Alan Bates). Dad was so flustered that in introdocing her, he briefly choked on Mom's name!

On arrival at Treasure Cay, they went to claim one of only three cottages on a miles-long beach. Theirs was in the middle of two other buildings, mere feet apart. Whilst they were being welcomed in the living room, a little boy of four or five years ran in from the beach, grabbed Dad around the knees, look up in his eyes, and called out "Daddy, Daddy!" Later Mom prepared Dad Beef Wellington. "Hmm," he thought, "She is not only wonderful, sweet, smart, and beautiful, but Jane can cook too!" Mom thought, "Wow, that was incredibly difficult. I hope I don't have to do that too often!" And they've been married for over fifty years since.

Ann Dillon Wachtmeister (née Wiberg), born in NYC in 1968. Ann was captain of Red House at Madeira, and one of the fastest swimmers in the Bahamas. Later active in the English Speaking Union, she was a debutante at the Waldorf Astoria with a Swedish escort "presenting" her. She obtained degrees at Pine Manor, the American College of London, and a Masters in Education from Trinity University in Washington, DC (her room mate was Fina, Sofia's sister). She is strong in languages, and has a natural gift for making people, particularly young people, feel at ease. Soon after meeting Atle Bekken, she not only learned the complex sport of polo, having not even been an equestrian, but she was so committed and accomplished that she is entrusted to manage a team!She teaches at Viktor Rydberg Gymnasium just outside Stockholm.

John Åke Wiberg, born 1969 in NYC, spent more time than any other of the second generation living at and repairing the Manor, something he still does. He also ran a boat named *Godzilla* setting mooringsin Nantucket, off New England. He has backpacked through Vietnam, Peru, Thailand, Laos, even northern Pakistan, with a beard and turban as a disguise. He cycled through Ireland and camped in snow and ice in New Hampshire, where he mastered snowboarding at Plymouth State. While at Franklin College, Switzerland, a classmate photographed John with a ponytail riding a horse outside the Hermitage in Leningrad! He runs his own building firm, and maintains the speed boat*Shoal Shaker* in tip-top condition. He loves fishing and taking the family boating.

Eric Troels Wiberg, born NYC 1970. Father of Felix, author of 10 books. As a sailor, has been on 4 round-the-world trips, worked on 118 boats or ships, 75,000 miles at sea (enough to circle the globe at the equator 3 times), been to 60+ countries or island groups,. In collegehe stayed awake 14 days on Ben & Jerry's *Chunky Monkey* ice cream, coffee and pizza while writing 4 books (then slept for 3 days). Lives in NYC, worked in yachts, tankers, tugs, newspapers, headhunting - all maritime. Started small ventures in reruiting, trucking, publishing, real estate and yacht delivery. Since high school has obtained certificates or degrees in law, marine affairs, script writing, and a combination of English and international studies from 6 universities in 3 countries and 3 states. He travels for work with a family tug-boat firm in NYC. Likes to communicate.

James McDermid Wiberg, born 1972 in NYC. Christened on a Swedish ship. Graduated from Rollins College in Florida, where he was close to his grandparents. At Cardigan Mountain School in New Hampshire we was so frustrated at not being able to cross country ski over snow that he mastered it, became team captain, and set a record! He earned a post-grad degree from London School of Economics with a paper on Freeport, Grand Bahama.

After earning Series 7 and other US licenses to trade stocks, he moved to Chicago, then back to Florida before returning to Nassau, where he met Aoife, through a Bacardi. She was supposed to return to Europe and he was to be assigned to Guatemala. That resulted in their getting married in Nassau. James has worked with Corner Bank on a very loyal tenure, and is president of the Bahamas Lawn Tennis Association. He is very active with the Hash House Harriers, a social and exercise group, and likes to explore the islands by mailboat.

Gustaf Carl Jacob Wachtmeister was born in Sweden in 1962. Around 1990 he and our first cousin, Magnus von Essen, lifelong friends and schoolmates, visited Nassau after a long round-world trip together in which they also visited Gustaf's uncle, Ambassador Willie Wachtmeister. He and Ann were married in the Spring of 1993. Gustaf is very much considered a brother to the *Bahama Wibergs*. He has a career in finance which has taken him to Oslo, London, Stockholm, Germany, Helsinki, and beyond. A graduate of Lundsberg Skola and Uppsala, he is married to Johanna (Sofia's dear friend), and they have a son. He is a member of the most exclusive hunting club of Sweden. Once Gustaf and I were perched in a hunting stand in Skåne, waiting confidently for the appearance of animals in the fields at evening. As darkness fell, Gustaf called his cousin, asking, "That fox you killed the other day, did you by any chance dump it under the hunting tower we are in?" Of course he had, and we shot nothing. Darn cousin!

Ann and Gustaf's three boys: Oscar Fredrik James Wachtmeister was born in London in 1994. Wilhelm Otto Anders followed in Stockholm in 1996, then Axel Gustaf Ericin 1998. All attended Carlssons Skola on Kommendörsgatan near Farmor's, followed by Lundsberg (third generation at least, Björke House). Oscar and Wilhelm have begun their studies at Lund. Axel is considering a career in the armed forces, Oscar in finance, and Wilhelm in shipping finance.

Satu Demientieff Wiberg, born in 1969 in Keuruu, Western Finland, was introduced to John by a friend of

Eric's in Singapore. She was working as purser (accounting officer) aboard Carnival Cruise Lines (the world's largest fleet), and their vessel called in Nassau on a weekly basis. After a fire damaged the vessel on which she worked, they were able to spend more time together. Satu works for a leading global travel agency, through which she is able to travel.

Henrik spent his early years in Finland, then in his mid-teens moved to Nassau with his John and Sofia, Oliver and Isabelle. Henrik has been a soccer star for his age group in Helsinki, even being offered scholarships to train at camps in Europe. His addition to the team in Bahamas has been a huge boost to them.

In this photo, Uncle Johnny looks like he is speaking on the phone with a foot! (In fact, it is his son Oliver's right foot – they are listening to Grandmommy telling stories at his grandparent's house).

 Sofia Johnson Wiberg was born in 1978 in Sweden, not far from the Norwegian border, in an area famous for its skiing. Her mother lived in the Bahamas for years and inspired many great paintings there. Her father was an engineer with the government.

Sofia studied the hotel and hospitality business in Switzerland among other places, and has worked aboard passenger vessels sailing internationally. As a result, she has a great network of friends around the globe and is also strong in languages.

Her half-sister Josefina (Fina) lives in Nassau and is an amazing aunt to their children. Fina is also a lifelong dear friend to Ann as well as the Wiberg boys (Bill Johnson was a writing mentor to Eric…..).

Sofia has a big job balancing the accounts at a major international design firm run in different countries and cities by our relative Amanda Lindroth, whose work has graced the cover of innumerable design publications globally. Her friend Johanna was maid of honor at their lovely beach wedding at Lyford Cay Marina – as we saw earlier, Johanna is Mama to Ann's son's half-brother! (Yes, it sometimes seems there are a lot of threads woven together…..).

This is Oliver John Wiberg, born 2009. He has lived and been educated in the Bahamas his whole life, but he returns to his Mom's home in Sweden every summer. He is active on and in the water, and also with boats and fishing. His family have three dogs – Skittles, Schooner, and Stitchy, and they also have a bird that likes to follow Oliver and Isabelle all over – inside the house. They used to have a goat named Maggie, but it ate all the fruits and grass, and so she now lives in a petting zoo. She was discovered on Eleuthera as a baby.

This is Isabelle Victoria Wiberg. She was born in 2012. Like her brother, there is a good chance she can obtain several citizenships! She is the third generation of Wiberg in the Bahamas. She also studies in Nassau. In this photo she is visiting her Farmor, or Grandmommy's house.

Felix with his Mom and Dad. Alexandra (Alex) Talmage (née Gray) Wiberg was born in 1970, the same week and in the same area as Eric! Though originally she was raised in Connecticut, soon her father's law work took them to the North Shore of Boston, where her Mom has lived since. Alex has two brothers. She has always loved animals, in part since she grew up on farms. In this photo she is holding a black labrador puppy Beckham. Felix has three pets on his bed each night (the fourth, Monkey the cat, is shy).

At home in Westport, she and Felix have two cats, Milo and Monkey, a black lab named Pinot Noir, and a pond with a wild duck named Lulu who introduces ducklings to Alex every spring. Alex studied at Dana Hall (same as her mother in law Jane!) as well as the University of Vermont. She has been certified as a massage therapist and ran her own business in Colorado. Growing up, she was a competetive three-day-event horseback rider. She is very astute at strategic board games, which is good, since so is Felix.

This is Felix Perkin Dunmore Wiberg, born in Stamford, Connecticut in 2007. His middle names are from Alex' family, as well as Dunmore Town, Harbour Island, where Eric and

Alex met and were engaged. Felix has lived in Norwalk, then Westport. For a few years he learned a little Hebrew at Temple Beth El, now he studies Chinese at Greens Farms Academy. He has always been interested in sports, music, and games of strategy.

He's played soccer goalie, fencing, and American football, where his is currently lineman on both sides, and dabbled in skating. He's played piano, trumpet, and tried drums. His interest in games is such that he often triumphs over his parents. He has a fictional nation named Belkin that he builds and defends with a friend. He even dictated a short book detailing his perspectives on Napoleon's strategies, (sounds like he and Farfar have a lot to talk about). Mostly, Felix likes to chill at home with family, friends, and his pets. He has already been to six countries, including Germany, Sweden, Norway, and Canada, and plays Xbox with one of his best friends, Max, who lives in Hong Kong. He is lucky to have a very devoted Grinnie, (Alex's Mom Winnie), as well as Godfathers Uncle Ted and Uncle John.

Dr. Aoife Houlihan Wiberg was born 1970 in Dublin to academic and medical parents who moved to England. Aoife obtained degrees in sustainable architecture at Cambridge and Cardiff, and took up a position at an architectural firm in Nassau. A schoolmate of her brother Finn's introduced her to James, who was beginning his career in finance. Rather than risk being separated, they decided to marry locally. In 2001 they were blessed with Saoirse Ada Jane Houlihan Wiberg (Ada for her Grandmum), and in 2003 with a son, Åke Finin Houlihan Wiberg (named for his Granddad and an uncle). Aoife holds a PhD as a tenured professor in Trondheim, Norway.

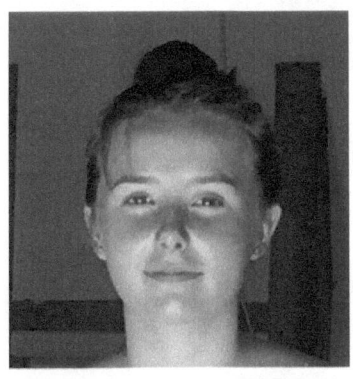

Saoirse's name is pronounced "sear-sha" and means freedom in Gaelic. She and Åke have lived a few places. After a few years they returned with their Mum to the UK, where Aoife resumed here PhD work in architecture at Cambridge. Then she accepted a professorship at Trondheim University in central Norway. The children learned Norwegian there, and befriended Eric's Singapore colleague, Harald Svensen, originally from Australia.

On top of six years in the Bahamas, Aoife has also worked in the UK, Ireland, Hong Kong, and Malaysia. Recently, another promotion beckoned, so the three moved to Berkley California for sabbatical. Åke began playing on the Junior Varsity American football team as a Freshman.  Saoirse joined a volleyball team, and is considering a scholarship to a European boarding school, so we will see!

Lynette S. Outten Wiberg was born in the Bahamas in 1983. Her family is originally from the Turks and Caicos Islands, which are adjacent to the Bahamas. Her family is so musical that for many years they had their own national radio program on ZNS, called the Outten Family, which would play live. Her father was on the Royal Bahamas Police Band for several decades and has played for many world leaders during the 1970s and 80s, including Gorbachev and Reagan. Her mother runs a church school program at their church, in whichh they are very active.

Lynette has worked very hard from Nassau to Houston to obtain degrees and licensesto become a pharmacist in the Bahamas That will open up many doors for her. James and Lynette were married at St. Christopher's Church in Lyford Cay. We understand that the stork may revisit their home and potentially bless them with another son early in 2018!

James with daughter Elizabeth at *Palmeiras*. Starting when we had fires in the fireplace, it was so cold, the *Bahamas Wibergs* have had Christmas Eve dinners with gift opening, prededed by a Santa Lucia party for the community.

James (right) with brothers Eric and John aboard the family boat, *Shoal Shaker*, summer of 2017.

Here are Anders William Wiberg, born in Nassau in 2014, and his adorable younger sister, Elizabeth, born in 2016. They share their home with two cats year-round, and in the summer with their half-sister Saoirse and half-brother Åke, for roughly six weeks, sometimes more.

They and their parents live along Skyline Drive, on the ridge behind Cable Beach and Goodman's Bay where a number of expatriates, from the Sigrists to the Wanklyns, the Duke and Duchess of Windsor, and other politicians (PM Pindling among them), and businessmen have lived. The US Ambassador keeps residence across the street, ensuring a degree of security, and the headquarters of the sitting Prime Minister are also located nearby.

Unfortunately, the construction of the golf course at Baha Mar starting about 2015 cut off direct access between Mom and Dad's home *Palmeiras* on Prospect Ridge and James and Lynette's home on Skyline Drive, however it only adds a matter of minutes to the drive.

NOTES: To learn more about our branch of the Wiberg family, visit the Facebook.com page dedicated to, and called *Bjära Släkten*. Though it is in Swedish, as family you are welcome to join, and you can count on replies to your queries in English. Or you can buy the 1950s version of the two-volume set of *Bjära Släkten* on Amazon.com, through specialist booksellers, or by asking a senior relative.

Further, you can go on Ancestry.com and look for family trees made by Magnus Lindroth, Eric Wiberg, or simply look for the *Wiberg, Lindroth, Fairbanks, McDermid* family tree. You will find a lot of information, and maybe add some of your own, as it is a highly cooperative, volunteer effort. If you are very serious, look up our distant Fairbanks cousin, Scott Steward, a genealogist at the New England Genealogical Society in Boston. He is an expert.

They say every family has someone who keeps the history – will you be that person?

PART II

PREFACE
(By author Mats Larsson)

Åke Wiberg is not among today's better-known figures in Swedish business circles. Yet in his heyday he was often a headliner in local and national Swedish media. His business empire encompassed a variety of operations from producing stockings to wood impregnation, and it employed several thousand people. Åke Wiberg's entrepreneurial spirit and drive made him successful in both business and politics.

Writing Åke Wiberg's biography has not always been an easy task. Much of the correspondence and other personal documents he left behind have been destroyed, and it has been necessary to search records from companies he owned and from other sources. I have received considerable assistance from a number of researchers, and I wish to thank them all, especially Maria Skarped at Loka Brunn; Deta Liljenfeldt at the Swedish National Arts Council; Anders Perlinge of the Stockholm Enskilda Bank archives at Täckaudden; and Professor Pontus Hellström and Steffan Wahlquist who generously granted us access to their private files.

In my work on this book I have had extremely valuable discussions with Göran Mörner, Åke Wiberg's colleague during his final years, and the Chairman of the Åke Wiberg Foundation. Göran has also been an inspirational teacher who helped me understand Åke Wiberg as a person. I have also received significant assistance from Lars Engvall, Peter Hedberg, Sven Jungerhem, Lars Jansson and Håkan Lindgren who proofread different entries and chapters and given me important insights. A special note of appreciation goes to Åke Wiberg's eldest son Anders Wiberg, who willingly made himself available during his trips to Sweden for our interviews.

THE FOUNDATION – INSTRUMENT OR MONUMENT?
(By Göran Mörner, Chairman of the Åke Wiberg Foundation)

Åke Wiberg is an unknown person for most people today. He passed away in 1963. On the other hand, his Åke Wiberg Foundation is fairly familiar to researchers, educators and humanitarian workers.

Sweden has a variety of fundraising, pension-based and family-oriented foundations - aside from a very large number of so-called charitable foundations, which are exempt from taxation. Most of Sweden's charitable foundations are relatively small and often limited to specific tax-free activities. The Åke Wiberg Foundation is one of the larger such institutions, estimated to be among the twenty largest charitable foundations in Sweden. Others, such as the Knut and Alice Wallenberg Foundation, or the Söderberg Foundation, are much bigger, while for example the Royal Jubileum Foundation is considerably smaller.

There are several explanations concerning the origins of charitable foundations in Sweden. Long before the Reformation of the 1500's wealthy families often donated major assets to cloisters or churches, such as land holdings under the condition that charitable contributions be made from them. In reality, churches usually came to regard these holdings as their own private property, and any incomes from them went straight to the churches themselves. After the Reformation these and other church properties were incorporated into the construction of a national state and its institutions.

During the 1500's and 1600's the earlier propensity to donate seems to have diminished, but not died. During the following centuries and into our own times the wealthy have steadily increased their gifts to various charitable causes. A dramatic rise in donations resulted from the breakthrough of industrialism and the significant amounts of capital accumulation which resulted from it.

Thusly, institutions resembling modern foundations became all the more common. We might ask which motives their creators had. An old insight appears to have survived: He who has been successful and become rich should share his wealth.

As society became more and more differentiated and social mobility increased, there was a growing risk that he who was no longer active in business nor politics would be soon forgotten. A desire to keep one's own name, or at least the family name, alive and in the public eye naturally evolved. A foundation was one effective way to accomplish this goal.

In 1947 and 1948 new income tax laws were enacted in Sweden. Direct taxation of incomes from work and capital could on this highly progressive scale reach up to 80 percent. On top of this came an estate tax which could result in total taxes of more than one hundred percent of an annual income.

At the same time the estate tax was complemented by a property tax as a kind of retroactive capital income tax, which added up to a total estate tax in extreme cases of up to 65 percent. This tax was even applied to gifts. The object of this tax system, which was described as history-making but was much more than just that, was primarily to provide the nation with the wherewithal for major social reforms. Another goal was the redistribution of society's resources for the benefit of its less fortunate citizens.

Economists and lawyers were engaged to find ways to avoid, or at least minimize, the effects of this new tax system. Many proposals were made, especially in the legal sphere. Creating foundations was one new measure – albeit an uncommon one – which resulted.

Descriptions of work done by Åke Wiberg in the 1930's and 1940's, often together with his brother and other family members, will soon follow. They opened a factory for stocking production (Malmö Strumpfabrik), a wood impregnation and refining company (Industrioch Byggnads AB Suecia), and then a commercial venture providing large tonnage ships with parts and supplies (AB Herman Gotthardt). These enterprises were all successful and contributed to the establishment of a stock portfolio, enabling the purchase of five urban properties in central Stockholm.

In addition, as of 1939 Åke Wiberg personally owned the Apertin Manor and estate in Värmland(which he renovated to the highest antique and operational standards) and a property named Bajonetten 6 – 8 on Strandvägen, where he had his Stockholm offices and living quarters. In the 1940's he helped his brother

Magnus acquire the Misterhult property in Småland, approximately 7,000 acres.

Parallel to Åke Wiberg's business ventures in the 1930's and 1940's, he was immersed in politics, first locally in Skåne and then in the Swedish Parliament.

Although this was probably more than most people could manage, he was also very active in cultural circles, on the boards of directors for the National Art Council, the Nordic Museum and the East Asian Museum. He also oversaw the restoration of Loka Brunn.

We are also going to describe later how Åke Wiberg, aside from his multiple business operations, supported charitable agencies, public service endeavors and political causes. He paid a heavy price, and his health suffered accordingly.

In 1953 Åke Wiberg designed a blueprint for the foundation which would come to bear his name. The foundation capital amounted to one million Swedish kronor, which were apparently paid in cash that year. This would amount to over 12.5 million kronor in today's world, and was no more than most other small foundations had at their disposal at that time.

The first years after its creation the foundation appears to have been dormant. Åke Wiberg most likely saw the foundation as a kind of security measure, one of several possible developmental alternatives.

It is also of note that during these years he was busy negotiating with a major Swedish bank. These negotiations appeared to involve a non-cash transfer of Wiberg family properties to an investment company closely allied to the bank. Åke Wiberg's probable intent was to gain access to the investment company's pending issue of new stocks. But talks ended over disagreement concerning the company's value.

Foundation holdings today include a stock portfolio worth about a billion kronor, and a wood impregnation company which functions as a specialty sawmill for lumber and related products - all worth from 5-10 percent of the foundation's capital. About two thirds of foundation stock dividends go to various medical research projects, while the rest support other humanitarian research, health care services and care, teaching support and education for children and youth. The foundation charter actually points out other unattended areas of support, but it is very safe to say that dividends cover a large amount of territory.

Fears of being unable to transfer his companies to the next generation, interests in an ability to continue supporting his prioritized causes, and his realization that his time on Earth was quite limited – any single factor provided enough motivation for creating a foundation, not to mention their combined effects.

Åke Wiberg, as we have said, was active economically, culturally and politically. As one of a few people outside the family who knew Åke Wiberg well and was a close working colleague during his final years, I would like to provide the following portrait of Åke Wiberg as an employer and private person.

Åke Wiberg was primarily characterized – aside from his remarkable intellectual abilities – by his intensity and determination, often accompanied by a certain restlessness and severe impatience. He owned a fascinating personal charm and knew quite well how to use it. His manner of thinking and attacking problems was keenly analytical, and often amazingly well-suited to future developments.

His work methods were well prepared and by the numbers. Åke Wiberg had an ability to delegate, but he never relinquished a strong hands-on control of operations. His excellent memory, even for relatively minor details, made his management style most effective. Even during his last ten years of bad health, when most people in his situation would have retired, he maintained the same working pace and routines as always.

But Åke could be surprisingly spontaneous, in both positive and negative situations. Positive ones were often associated with some forms of generosity, while negative ones could be very unnerving for the persons targeted.

The relaxation that Åke Wiberg allowed himself often stemmed from his cultural activities and included a great interest in older art forms, in antiquities and in the continual restoration and renovation of the Apertin Manor and estate and of his home in Stockholm.

Åke Wiberg's personal qualities were such that no one who interacted with him could remain indifferent to him. Those who worked closely with him often felt a great loyalty.

Let me describe an example of what kind of impression Åke Wiberg could make on folks outside his inner circle of family and friends. A newly appointed Supreme Commander of the Swedish Armed Forces, Helge Jung, had been in contact with parliamentarian Åke

Wiberg. He asked Minister of Defense Per Edvin Sköld what he thought about Wiberg. Jung said "Wiberg is very young, very gifted and he knows exactly what he wants."

Åke Wiberg was an innovator. He had strong ties to his family. He was forward-looking, at times visionary. He wanted to protect everything he had built up against the ravages of temporary fiscal interests. He was generous. And he certainly did not wish to be forgotten.

All the usual motivations for the establishment of a foundation which would carry forward Åke Wiberg's name and life's work were definitely in place.

We have already seen above that, according to the standards of our times, Åke Wiberg was an exceptional human being. Within the circles of those who are active in his foundation and therefore responsible for the continued development of his life's work, there is general agreement that he was a person of the highest dignity, and the era of his operations is of great interest to a large number of people.

This is why this document, this memorial to Åke Wiberg, has been undertaken.

CHILDHOOD AND YOUTH
(By author Mats Larsson)

Åke Wiberg's family on his paternal side came from the Kristianstad area, where both his great-great-grandfather and great-grandfather farmed the old family fields. Great grandfather Ola Jeppsson was born in 1802, and in 1824 he married Elna Trulsdotter, whose father owned one of the region's largest farms. The couple had six sons and two daughters, and their plan was surely that one of their sons would take over their farm. But one after another the sons chose to enter Lund University and then pursue other non-agricultural vocational paths.

Ola Jeppsson certainly misjudged his sons' interest in farming, but by mortgaging the farm and selling it lot by lot he could assist his sons in their chosen employs. The eventual consequences were devastating for the Jepson's, who left this Earth with neither farm nor appreciable assets.

The best known of Ola Jeppsson's sons was Martin Wiberg, who completed his doctorate in philosophy at Lund and then devoted himself to his inventions. They were not especially technologically advanced, but included the letter box which the Swedish Post Office used throughout the 20th century, as well as an early model of a rotating adding machine. Another of Ola Jeppsson's sons, Truls Wiberg, moved to Gothenburg after completing his studies at Lund and became a teacher at Gothenburg's Latin High School.

Thus, a branch of the Wiberg family had left Skåne to seek its fortune in Gothenburg. A high school teacher's salary was indeed modest, but through smart real estate purchases in rapidly growing Gothenburg, Truls was able to live quite comfortably. He also bought a farm in Marks Harad which eventually became the family's summer home.

Truls and Elna had two daughters and five sons. When Truls was only 38, he died, leaving Elna alone with seven children. The family lived for a short time in Stockholm, but returned to Gothenburg where the youngest sons, Yngve and Hjalte, lived with their mother. They were a close-knit family unit, and Truls' and Elna's seven children were also close. For example, Truls and Elna both chose to attend Gothenburg Latin High School (later named Hvitfeldiska Gymnasium) where Truls taught mathematics and other subjects until 1888. One of the many Wiberg cousins who went there in the early 1900's was Yngve Åberg's eldest son Åke.

Yngve Wiberg was born in the middle of an economic boom period in 1873, and was only 15 when his father died in 1888. He attended high school for a while in Stockholm, but he completed his studies at Gothenburg Latin. He went on to Chalmers Technical Institute where he earned an engineering degree. Yngve, together with his younger brother Hjalte, acquired a company with connections to the leather industry, AB Göteborgs Gamla Trätoffelfabrik (Old Clog Factory).

In the mid-1890's Yngve was offered the directorship of Stillefors Träförädling AB (Wood

Refinement) outside of Jönköping. This was quite an honor for an engineer in his early 20's, and he accepted the job. This did have an impact on the clog company the two brothers were managing. Up until that time, Yngve had been the primary force in the firm, but he could hardly run that show from Jönköping.

The brothers decided to continue owning the company, but Hjalte would take over control of the operation. In the ensuing future, Yngve was still involved and often went to Gothenburg. As for Stillefors, Yngve was at first a hired director, but after a few years he acquired stock in the company and became its sole owner.

A young, single businessman, Yngve Wiberg was an admired addition to Jönköping society, and was often a guest at the estates in the area. At a trial in the regional court in Jönköping his eyes fell upon the lovely young Thyra Flodin. Before he had even been introduced to her he told a friend "That's the girl I'm going to marry. Do you know who she is?"

He was later introduced not only to Thyra, but also to her parents, Josephine and Johan Magnus Flodin. They approved of Yngve Wiberg and invited him to visit at the Flodin family manor, Dalskogssäteri. Yngve courted their daughter as was the custom then, and after a while they were engaged. Their wedding was on August 19, 1899. The following year their first child, Margot, was born.

Owning and running two companies was very demanding, and limited Yngve's time with his growing family. The newlyweds stayed at Stillefors until 1902, but Yngve decided to sell the company and move to

Gothenburg to devote all his efforts to the expanding clog and wood operations there.

Back in Gothenburg, the family settled into their home in the city center, or in their house in Malevik by the Särö rails, which carried the trains between Gothenburg and Särö. Their family grew, and as years went by they had four children. After Margot, Åke was born in 1902, Magnus in 1903 and finally Cajsa in 1914. Back in Gothenburg, Yngve Wiberg concentrated his energy on the company he and his brother Hjalte had built up. As for Hjalte, he left after a few years to work with the Swedish subsidy of an international oil company. So Yngve was now alone in leading the company he and Hjalte had created, and through mergers operations expanded to new business areas.

The basis of Yngve Wiberg's business model was the wood-clog factory the brothers had acquired in Gothenburg. Production of boots and shoes grew before World War 1, but wartime meant a lack of materials, forcing them to employ simpler raw materials and construction methods. The use of wooden soles became more and more widespread, not only in clogs and boots, but in common shoes as well. Thick Argentine leather was replaced by cheaper qualities and substitutes. Direct sales to private consumers and orders from varied government agencies maintained decent sales results during the war.

There was also interest in Swedish footwear from the Germans, as their access to shoe leather diminished. In early 1915 German officials contacted Yngve Wiberg with a tempting business proposition. They wanted to finance a large-scale manufacture of wooden shoe soles for export to Germany. The Germans assumed all economic risks, but they needed someone to run the operation, and Yngve

Wiberg's experience made him the right candidate for that job.

Wiberg would do this work on top of his ordinary company duties, and he'd receive an annual salary of SEK 100,000 (ca SEK 4 million = $450,000 in today's currency) plus other benefits. All necessary raw materials, machinery and know-how were available in Sweden, and through Wiberg's contacts with wood producers in Småland they could begin operations quickly. At the outset of the war there was a strong pro-German opinion in Sweden, so the Swedish government had no objections to the plan.

This was indeed a tempting offer for Yngve Wiberg, but he turned it down directly, and apparently not for political reasons. He felt his family was doing well enough to meet all its needs and provide his children with a proper academic education. Building up an operation which would disappear after the war was in no way in line with Yngve Wiberg's business philosophy.

Yngve Wiberg does not appear to have been an especially adventure-some businessman. He was not one of his era's opportunists who tried to profit from the speculative wave that swept over Sweden during the war. The Wiberg companies were hit hard by deflationary crises in the early 1920's. Competition increased greatly after the war, and prices fell. When higher quality products hit the market, they could no longer sell the simple shoes and boots they produced during the war.

They had to throw away and burn a major portion of the supplies of raw materials they had accumulated during the war years, and many of Yngve Wiberg's companies lost money and went bankrupt. But in contrast to what was the case in other manufacturing sectors, it was relatively easy to return to shoemaking for the Swedish market, since the footwear industry in the 1920's and 1930's was protected by tariffs on imported goods

By 1920 Åke Wiberg was still just a teenager, but we can assume that he got to learn a lot from his exposure to his father's business work. We can sense Åke's high opinion of his father as a person and as a business leader if we read the letters he wrote in the 1950's and 1960's. He mentions, among other things:

"Yngve was a noteworthy personality, independent and a man of principle. He had strong opinions, sympathies and antipathies. People knew they could trust what he said. We can say without exaggeration that he was a competent and reliable man with good judgement, and that he fully deserved his fine reputation as a person, and a born leader."

Åke Wiberg was apparently quite close to his father, but whether these feelings arose in childhood, or later on when he came to appreciate and admire Yngve as an entrepreneur with a strong personality, is a matter of conjecture. As an adult, Åke Wiberg shared the same strong family attachments that Yngve had. This is reflected in their mutual interest in documenting their family history.

Åke Wiberg's descriptions in his books of his dad Yngve are much more vibrant and complex than those of his mother Thyra. Certain of Yngve's characteristic features seemed to appeal especially to Åke. Several times in Åke's family chronicles he points out his father's ability to attack problems and analytically solve them through hard work. The following passage demonstrates this:

"It was never difficult for Yngve to get to the point of something, and he was not a man of sweeping gestures. He was used to his surroundings, and he got to the heart of the matter steadily and calmly. Naturally, like anyone else, he made mistakes, but he was the first to admit it and to recognize a better solution. He once said that those who work a lot make a lot of mistakes, and if anyone is worth suspicion, it's he who never seems to make one."

As a sole proprietor and owner of a small business empire, Åke Wiberg naturally had his reasons to emphasize his admiration for Yngve the entrepreneur when he penned his family biographies in the 1950's. Yngve's capacity to work assuredly made him a role model for his son Åke Wiberg.

In his youth, Åke Wiberg was close to his uncle Hjalte and his family. Yngve and Hjalte were Truls' youngest offspring, the afterthoughts. They fortunately found good company in each other. The mutual company they owned brought them even closer together. Their families were also very close during Åke's childhood and later on. Åke seemed to especially appreciate Hjalte's sense of humor and playfulness, which Yngve did not have.

Åke's younger brother Magnus came to mean a lot to him as time passed. They naturally spent their childhood together and attended the same school for a few years. But while Åke continued his studies at the University of Lund, Magnus chose to leave high school at the age of sixteen. This could have cut off their relationship, but quite to the contrary they came to work very closely with each other.

When Magnus left school, he went to work at his father's clog factory and entered night school in order to improve his education skills. Eventually he took business courses which he put to good use in their company.

Magnus began working on the factory floor, both to gain product knowledge and to understand the manufacturing process. As time passed he would accompany his father on sales trips and got to practice his customer skills, as well as practical office work, budgeting, accounting and tax questions. Since he began work at his father's factory in 1921, he experienced firsthand how companies could be affected by economic problems. The economic slowdown which hit Sweden and other countries from 1921 to 1923 was one of the worst depressions of the 20th century. His father, and the crisis of the 1920's, taught Magnus to avoid taking major economic risks. Once again, Åke Wiberg saw his father as a model businessman and company pioneer.

"Our father had a very positive influence on Magnus's general view of how a businessman should act. For their entire lives they were adept at avoiding contact with certain people, and judging which persons you could really depend upon. My brother always lived by a rule which said that any deal should be such that it gave an advantage to both parties. Temporary favors were not something to strive for. A salesman intended that his customers would be satisfied in the long run. Maybe it was this business mentality, which Magnus learned early on, which allowed him to feel a special connection to our English contacts."

Magnus assumed more and more responsibility for Gothenburg's Old Clog and Wood Company. The market for their products got weaker with time, and the family was discussing the establishment of new operations in markets other than footwear. In the 1930's Yngve and Magnus Wiberg together started a wholesale firm, Wima Fabriks AB. With Magnus as president, the company grew to a turnover of about five million kronor. By the close of the 1930's Magnus had assumed the leadership of both Gothenburg companies when he was recruited to join the group of businesses that Åke Wiberg was putting together. This meant that the two brothers would be in constant contact with each other.

THE SCHOOL YEARS

In 1909 Åke Wiberg entered Gothenburg's Seminariet grammar school, where many of the city's wealthiest families sent their children. As was often the case back then in Sweden, the classes had a religious orientation. Åke's first teacher there placed great emphasis upon the Christian message, and every Monday he expected that his students would be able to report back on what was said in Sunday's mass and evening song the previous day. The younger children divided up the church visits between themselves and met before school to review what had been said there. The tough discipline and religious upbringing made this teacher anything but popular.

After those first two years in the old Seminariet building, the school was relocated to the former college quarters on The Avenue, across from Stora Teatern, where the school remained during the years Åke Wiberg went there. As most students lived near Linneplatsen, this now involved a rather long way to go for the students. The city trolleys were a luxury which students were seldom able to use. They walked to school. This was before schools served any meals, and the long school days meant that most children took sandwich lunches with them.

After three years at Seminariet, Åke Wiberg entered his father's high school, Gothenburg Latin High.

As the name suggests, student studies were Latin-centered, and in 1939 a more natural sciences-based course of studies began. It was only natural for the Wiberg children to attend Gothenburg Latin, and in the following years (1910 to 1920) ten Wiberg cousins graduated from Latin. The Latin course lines were primarily language and humanities subjects, but the school had basic mathematics studies as well. Åke Wibergs grandfather, Truls Wiberg, had been a lecturer there in the 1800's. Memories of him were still there from 1910 to 1920:

"The teachers of bygone times were so original, with such unique personalities, that modern times can hardly imagine them. Circumstances and rhythms of life were more fertile somehow. We had naturally a number of such teachers, the memories of whom have etched themselves indelibly into our minds. They were Carlbom, Kalle Meathead, Plumpy and many others. The stories about them are beyond counting. Our homeroom teacher one year was the old mathematician Hedelius, aka Skvapan. His grandfather was a teacher, and he spoke with great reverence about Old Truls."

Any Wiberg who made mistakes in mathematics was immediately reminded that much more was expected of the offspring of such a distinguished and gifted mathematician as grandfather.

A great deal of Åke Wiberg's time in high school was politically and economically dominated by the First World War. Before the war broke out, Åke's dad was active in the so-called Land Storm, where older students were to be considered for military service. It was only a theory on paper at the start, but when the war began, students were called in for an obligatory five-day training program. The training soon was discontinued, only to be reinstated in 1936. Land Storm's tasks became much clearer, as the need for border security and coastal defenses grew.

The Land Storm commanders were recruited from volunteers, and Yngve Wiberg was among them. As assistant section leader, and later section leader, he went through more days of training, finally advancing to platoon leader, comparable to a lieutenant's rank. A day after the war began, August 2, 1914, Sweden mobilized. Land Storm's men were called in to receive arms. In the cities, one could see them as well as regular military recruits. Yngve Wiberg's troops gathered at Heden outside of central Gothenburg – where his family even rented a cottage that summer. The troops were later deployed and camped along Säve Brook. Right after the war began, Yngve Wiberg was mobilized for several months, but since it was soon clear that Sweden was not facing any direct invasion threat, many of the Land Storm volunteer recruits were sent back home.

For a twelve-year-old Åke this must have been a frightening and exciting time. Several times he visited his father's camp quarters along Säve Brook, and Yngve had plenty of stories to tell about Land Storm happenings. We can assume that Åke Wiberg's interest in the nation's defense and in volunteer movements defending the country was awakened during this period. He was able to follow the Land Storm, and seems to have appreciated its importance. During the late 1930's and Second World War, Åke Wiberg supported Sweden's volunteer defense forces with financial contributions.

In June of 1920, Åke Wiberg graduated from Gothenburg's Latin High School. Judging by his grades, he had not been a devoted student. In languages –

Swedish, Latin, German, English and French – he only got a B, which was acceptable but not very impressive. His Swedish final essay on Verner von Heidenstam's poetry earned him an A- to B+, but his oral exam only resulted in a B. Åke was by no means bad at languages, on the contrary. Many of his classmates got the same results as he did. He received a B in Christianity and history, and in the natural sciences he averaged an A-. His best grades came in gymnastics and weapon exercises, where he earned an A. All in all, Åke Wiberg was a very average high school student.

After high school it was time to improve his command of languages and get some experience in the business world. Regardless of what Åke would end up doing in the future, getting involved in business was vital for getting an understanding of people and life at work. Business leaders in the major Swedish cities (Stockholm, Gothenburg, Malmö) often sent their children to either England or France, but the most common destination for apprenticeships was probably Germany.

In spite of the difficult situation during and after the war, there was still an interest in Sweden for things German. Germany was one of Sweden's most important trade partners, and business relationships were comprehensive. With Yngve's assistance, a 1920 summer apprenticeship for Åke was arranged at a paper factory on the German – Polish border. A series of documents helped prepare his journey to Germany. The area was being administrated by France, as Europe waited for new borders to be drawn up.

Both the trip itself and the new work must have been very exciting for the recent graduate, who had no significant previous experience in international travel.

During the war, the factory had been partially manned by Russian and Polish prisoners of war, later replaced by local Germans and Poles. The factory work was very heavy, and in shifts with low wages. And the living conditions were not ideal in a region still scarred by the war.

The apprenticeship provided not only insights into how paper was manufactured, but it developed Åke's language ability. He had studied German for nine years in school, but his conversational skills were very limited. But his command of basic grammar rules and his good vocabulary knowledge were in place, and with daily practice he was able to get along.

The following summer Åke Wiberg got the opportunity to test his skills again. He represented his father's shoe company in Sachsen in order to analyze the German leather industry's ability to provide high quality products at a reasonable price. At this time, Swedish leather suppliers were struggling with deflation and business slowdowns resulting from the First World War.

AT THE UNIVERSITY OF LUND

We have already noted that Åke Wiberg had a knack for natural science studies in school, while he had a much tougher time in language classes. At the same time, he was very fond of arts and literature, and he was careful to express himself correctly in oral and written form. He was barely twenty when his interest in a political career began to grow, but to succeed in that field he had to have a good education and contacts within Sweden's political establishment.

Aside from the humanities, Åke had an early interest in the social sciences, especially in law. Here there was a family tradition already in place. Several Wibergs of previous generations – some in Åke's – had completed legal studies. In the early 1920's legal studies were only available in Stockholm, Uppsala and Lund, so it was no surprise that Åke chose to study in Lund. He had no contacts there, but his family roots and their personal attachment to Skåne had been important to him since childhood.

In 1920 Åke graduated from high school and registered at the University of Lund. He took many courses in law, and also studied economics. By Christmas of 1921, he had rapidly secured a bachelor's degree in political science, with a major in economics.

As a new college student, Åke Wiberg was obliged to do his military service. He signed up as a draftee at the naval station in Karlskrona, but he apparently had no abiding interest in military life. He signed off as a petty officer and never considered continuing in the navy.

Back in Lund, he resumed his law studies and gained his law degree in 1924. During his years in Lund, Åke Wiberg had his first exposure to political life. His interests and convictions since childhood coincided with the right wing AVF party. Political activities were a way to make friends and meet people with similar values, and Åke immediately joined SNU, the Swedish National Youth Union, a wing of the AFV. But considering the serious university study load he was carrying, he must have had very limited time for any political work.

While Åke was living and studying in Lund he met his first wife, Märta Holmström, who was born in 1905 in Malmö and was studying medicine at the University of Lund. Her career choice was by no means easy. Back then, women doctors were both uncommon and (in some quarters) undesirable. She met opposition from the structure of the university itself and from many individual teachers. But Märta Holmström, whose intelligence and determination had a lot in common with Åke's, fought back against all those opposing her. Before she turned 30 she graduated from the University of Lund with a Doctorate of Medicine degree.

FAMILY AND NATIONAL POLITICS

When Åke Wiberg met his wife-to-be, Märta Holmström, during their studies in Lund, both felt it was important to complete their studies before they started a family. They did not get married until 1931, and by then Åke Wiberg's careers in politics and in business were well under way. Their first child, a son named Anders, was born in 1935, and then came Ann in 1938, and Jan in 1941.

Åke Wiberg had maintained close contact with people in Germany, but when he visited the country after Hitler's ascent to power in the mid 1930's, he was struck by how the country had changed character. The atmosphere was more severe, the militarism was obvious. This, combined with the Allied countries' policy of appeasement to Hitler made it clear to Åke Wiberg that a new European war was in the making. Increased tensions threatened Sweden, but especially Skåne, because of its proximity to Germany.

If war broke out and Sweden was drawn into it, there was a clear risk that large cities such as Malmö would be bombed from the air. Therefore, all small children should be evacuated from the city. This is why Åke Wiberg in the mid-1930's began searching for a farming and forestry property to which one could evacuate mothers and children. Many families were doing the same thing.

Many Skåne upper class families were also seeking properties to retreat to during the latter half of the 1930's. For Åke it was also important to be able to leave the city behind and come out to relax in the country. As he grew up, he often stayed with his uncle and his grandparents on their farms, and he became very fond of country life. By the mid-1930's Åke Wiberg's work load was such that he had a real need to get away and 'charge up his batteries.'

Åke had a truly systematic way of finding the right country property. He describes it himself as follows:

"At the start of 1936 we resided in Malmö, and we decided to try to acquire a small wooded property that was not too far away. I dictated a *promemoria*[diplomatic memo] where I described what our ideal place would look like.

It would be a farm with a small cultivated area, but hopefully a large amount of forestation. It should have a cottage or a house which would be liveable for us, and which would be located beside a lake. It may not lie further away than a two-hour drive by car from Malmö.

I sent this description with a questionnaire to all the banks and real estate offices in areas where there could be properties which met these conditions."

Through these contacts and advertisements in several newspapers, Åke Wiberg rapidly received a number of interesting replies. The countryside was being abandoned in Halland and Småland, and there were many farms for sale for relatively little money. So Wiberg made a number of visits to properties within the proper distance from Malmö. Many of these properties were of interest, but none was exactly what he was searching for. Then one day a banker from Halmstad called and said that he just found an object which could surely fit Åke's bill. It was named Attavara and was a few kilometers outside of Simlångs-dalen, near the border between Halland and Småland.

The property included several hundred acres of forest, but only six to eight acres of arable land. The farmhouse and storage barns were in good condition, and the purchase included a relatively new and well positioned house. Both the farm area and new house were very close to Attavara Lake."

At dawn one late spring morning Åke and has father Yngve drove out from Malmö to see Attavara for the first time. "We did not take the road through Simlångsdalen. Instead, we took the road through the forest to the south, which afforded us a first view of Attavara from the heights on the other side." Åke continued:

"That was how we met Attavara. At very first sight, the whole place was enchanting. The value of money was totally different from today, but the asking price included furniture, boats, equipment and everything you'd need for a weekend retreat. I accepted their offer immediately, and we filled in the sales contract."

In his descriptions of the Simlångsdalen area in general - and specifically Attavara – Åke Wiberg waxed naturally romantic. In his book about Attavara, he assumes the role of a regional wanderer who pauses to admire lovely scenery and carefully records everyday events in nature and in people's lives. He was visibly impressed by the hard work that many folks in this area carried out.

Åke did not intend to put the farm to any agricultural use. He was primarily interested in using the new house out by the lake for his family. He could easily lease out his fields for farming by others. Most of the property around Attavara Lake belonged to his farm. There were three other farms on the far side of the lake which had parcels bordering on the water. The forested parcels were not of any particular value, but they could be sold to accommodate several lakeside houses.

This was a danger to Åke Wiberg, because it could disturb the quiet lake environment. He then contacted the owners across the lake to discuss purchasing those lakeside parcels. They refused directly, but were willing to sell the entire three farm properties. Åke did not intend to expand his agricultural holdings, but the price was right and it would be possible to lease out these fields. So, he purchased the three farms. If the family ever wished to leave Attavara it would be possible to make a considerable profit by selling the lakeside parcels individually.

As the family grew, more living quarters were needed, since both friends and relatives often came to Attavara to visit. A new guest cottage with a panoramic view across the lake and a large garage was built in the late 1930's. It provided plenty of living space and offered the most modern comforts the 1930's had to offer anywhere.

In retrospect, these purchases appear to have been part of a very conscious strategy, as Åke expected that a major European war was looming. The renovation at Attavara was parallel to attempts to rationalize harvesting in agriculture and in forestry. Lands were drained off, and then plowed under and sown, or prepared for trees, as modern forestry was becoming more rational and manageable.

For Åke Wiberg, 1938 was a transitional year. The Attavara farm was not simply a rallying point for the stressed out big city family. Given the ever-increasing threat of war, Attavara was a strategically important place for Åke Wiberg and his closest friends to be near.

He gave a political speech in the spring of 1938 where he expressed not only his fears about circumstances in foreign countries, but he went to an uncommonly open attack – for a business leader – against Germany and its leader.

"Austria, our noble old friend, is at the end of a rope. The country has been violently forced into a foreign straightjacket. Attempts to disguise this with a plebiscite are given no excuse for what has happened. Does anyone believe that a plebiscite could ever result in a majority against German occupation? Is there anyone who believes that a free plebiscite which confirmed Austria's right to be a sovereign nation would lead Hitler to withdraw his German occupying troops out of respect for the voters? The plebiscite is and remains immaterial. Its forced results are known in advance, and Hitler cannot mesmerize the eyes of the world with his blue fairy dust."

But Åke Wiberg did not only criticize the German subjugation of Austria. In a most foresighted way, he warned what the future could have in store for other countries in the vicinity of Germany.

"The Nazi party, forbidden in Austria, and other German agents have been working silently in the shadows. The Nazis are acting much as they did as when Hitler carried out his successful coup in Germany. This should serve as a warning for other countries whose turn may be just around the corner. Or does anyone believe that this same subversive activity is not going on in Czechoslovakia? We can be quite sure that the Germans have a detailed plan for how they will carry out a coup in Czechoslovakia, who their opposition is, and which ones will be executed in order for the lightning-fast strike to paralyze the country."

As for Czechoslovakia's fate, Åke Wiberg's prediction came true in the fall of 1938, when parts of Czechoslovakia's Sudetenland were annexed into Germany. The entire country followed in March 1939. Czech annexation by German expansionism cannot have been a surprise for politically aware observers. But Åke Wiberg saw a real danger that the Nordic countries could be the victims of German espionage and military attack. In a speech in the spring of 1938, he also made clear references to both Russian ambitions and what he understood to be the German mentality:

"It is pointless to deny that our relationship to Germans is extremely distant, and that we will never be able to understand them, just as they will never learn to think the way we do. Discipline to the death, ruthless aggression, extreme stinginess, huge gestures, egoistic chauvinism and intense materialism are German values which are and should continue to be foreign to the Swedish way of thinking."

"Get rid of German influence. Let us begin this housecleaning immediately. We are not searching for disputes with Germany, but we demand now and in the future to preserve the peace which everyone respects, and will always protect against any enemy, Russian or German. If we were to find ourselves facing the same threat as Austria and perhaps other countries, we are fully prepared to do everything in our power to protect our democracy, our country, our people and our freedom."

Åke Wiberg clearly explained his national points of view, and exaggeration appears to have been a way to gain his listeners' full attention. This shows at the same time his clear opposition to Nazi politics and his will to strengthen Sweden's defenses.

Taking into account the political views which Åke espoused, it is not surprising that his family as early as 1938 had begun stocking up on vital supplies at Attavara. They also purchased more beds and covers in case the war made necessary to provide housing for more families on the farm. Especially after the Munich Agreement between Chamberlain and Hitler, the pace of gathering extra supplies at Attavara increased, and by New Year they had enough beds, bedclothes and supplies for twenty women and children at the new lake house. Åke, with his usual timely thoroughness, made up a list of the evacuated families they would receive at Attavara.

The outbreak of war in September of 1939 did not involve any large-scale population shifts. But when German initiated invasions of Norway and Denmark on April 9, 1940, the chosen families moved out to Attavara. During the following months there were twenty to twenty-five mothers and children staying there as evacuees.

CULTURE, POLITICS AND CONTACTS

Åke Wiberg devoted a good portion of the last twenty years of his life to cultural endeavors. As early as the dawning 1940's he was very active as an art collector and patron of the arts. When he was appointed board chairman of the Swedish National Arts Council in 1944, he was able to combine his art collecting and financial contributions with politics.

Åke Wiberg's command of how political decisions were made, and his personal relationships with politicians from many parties, were a significant advantage for the various cultural projects he oversaw. These were, above all, major influences from an economic perspective. All the cultural institutions that Wiberg worked with were suffering financially, and he could serve as a political door-opener in their striving to increase their funding efficiency.

His solid associations with industrial concerns and their representatives could also have positive influences upon cultural institutions. But Åke Wiberg seldom went to business colleagues and begged for contributions. He probably found such a position as embarrassing, given his own financial resources.

The cultural issues were so important to Åke that he had no problems in working with politicians from other parties. This became very clear during his work with the National Arts Council where he energetically defended the idea behind the creation of the Arts Council, which was originally introduced by Social Democratic minister of education and ecclesiastical affairs Arthur Engberg.

In contrast with Åke's work on the National Arts Council, his efforts for Loka Brunn, the Swedish Institute, the Labranda Committee and the East Asian Museum all involved his connections with the Swedish royal family. Åke Wiberg's initial close contacts with the royal court were via the office of the Marshall of the Realm in 1948, when he was appointed both as manager of Loka Brunn and as a board member of the Athens Institute in Athens, Greece. His personal contacts with the king were obviously something he valued immensely.

After Åke Wiberg left the national political stage in 1950, he divided his time between the management of his own business groups and his various cultural endeavors. This meant that he was at times deeply involved in projects very close to his heart.

THE ÅKE WIBERG FOUNDATION

The advent of the Industrial Revolution in the United States and in Europe led to the creation of a number of foundations dedicated to education and research. In Germany, two major foundations for scientific research were formed, the Humboldt Foundation in 1860 and the Carl-Zeiss Foundation in 1889. Two leading American foundations came as the new century dawned, The Carnegie Foundation in 1911 and the Rockefeller Foundation two years later.

The most internationally renowned Swedish foundation is without a doubt the Nobel Foundation, established through Alfred Nobel's will and testament in 1895. The goal of this foundation is to reward those whose research leads to significant progress, but it does not often create the conditions necessary to carry out such research. This is the very aim of the Knut and Alice Wallenberg Foundation, born in 1917.

Knut Wallenberg, an inheritor of the Stockholms Enskilda Bank (SEB), built up an enormous personal fortune from 1880 to 1900. When the foundation was formed he had about SEK 55 million, and he donated about half of it to the budding foundation. The foundation received continuous capital contributions, and its net worth in 2000 was over 22 billion kronor, making it the largest publicly owned Swedish foundation dedicated to research and education.

The years between the wars produced relatively few foundations, partially due to slow economic growth. More educational and research foundations appeared after WWII, especially during the industrial boom years of the 1950's and 1960's. Of the twenty largest foundations in 2002, seven arose during these decades.

The establishment of foundations in the early 1900's and after World War II appears to have been based on American models. American foundations have historically played a vital role in the economy. Successful people are expected to donate a portion of their capital holdings to publicly beneficial causes, to legitimize their capital accumulation and to compensate society for the successes it has enabled them to enjoy.

The Åke Wiberg Foundation was created in 1953, following an extended visit by Åke Wiberg in the USA. It seems likely that the creation and organization of his foundation was influenced by his time there and the contacts he had with American charitable agencies. But his foundation origins also reflected general charitable giving by leading Swedish industrialists, including foundation-maker's Torsten and Ragnar Söderberg and Axel Wenner-Gren.

The primary goals of those foundations created from 1950 to 1970 were to support research in Sweden. This was a period when Swedish industry was growing rapidly. Especially Swedish manufacturers – who often took advantage of home country innovations – contributed to building up Sweden's high standard of living. Scientific and technical research came to embody the pillars of Sweden's economy. So, it is no wonder that Sweden's industrial leaders gladly provided the resources for domestic research projects.

Åke Wiberg, when involved in his arts patronage work in the 1940's, showed a keen interest in science and culture. It is no surprise that these areas would be front and center in the new foundation charter, where the goal of the foundation's operations is:

"...to cooperate with Swedish military and/or other authorities to strengthen the national defense; to aid indicated families or other persons and encourage the care and upbringing of children; to provide support and preparation for teaching and education, and to make assistance available to those in need; and...to promote scientific research."

The organization of the foundation's charter was very much in line with Åke Wiberg's own interests. The charter's contents were directly lifted from regulations in the city tax laws and estate tax laws which exempted donors from taxes. Tax exemptions for certain publicly important companies were already recognized in the 1940's – as a new tax system was inaugurated – as vital to private charitable activities and their future.

Foundations also became a tool for business owners to fortify their family's future control over their companies. Inheritance taxes were so steep that company groups would have to be divided up and sold when in-family succession was at hand. The political left considered these public interest foundations to be an ownership tool used to create opaque power structures and therefore avoid taxes. A more positive view of foundation creation was that it was the only way for private citizens to directly contribute to the public good. Private foundations balanced the federal financing against their own cultural and research priorities.

The Åke Wiberg Foundation also had a capital management function. Through a company called Borgen, a major part of the ownership and control of the industrial operations and investment portfolio which was built up around Malmö Strumpfabrik (MSF) was transferred to the foundation. When Åke Wiberg died in 1963, his foundation was therefore the controlling owner of a small industrial empire.

The transfer of Wiberg's assets to the foundation can be viewed as a way of preserving the unity of the company group. When combined with Wiberg's interests in culture, science and charities, foundation control of these assets can be seen as a natural step for Wiberg. His family, however, was hit hard. A large part of that wealth which Åke Wiberg had built up disappeared from the family and landed in the foundation's accounts. Even if his family – especially the children – had other opinions than their father about this, protesting would have been futile. Given Åke Wiberg's determination and powers of persuasion, things would still end up as he had planned.

The creation of the foundation was undeniably due to Åke Wiberg's wish to keep the group's companies, which he had built up, together as they faced taxes which could eradicate them if he were to die. His generally negative opinion concerning high taxes was key here. And a foundation would serve as a monument to his contributions to society. This was also a major motivation for the foundation.

The creation of the foundation did not appreciably alter Åke Wiberg's control of his businesses. His central position in the foundation, and in many of his companies, kept him in the captain's chair until his death.

A LONG, DRAWN OUT ILLNESS

Åke Wiberg suffered through serious health problems from his early thirties on. They became more and more disturbing with time, and are the main reason he quit politics in 1949. The first symptoms came in 1935, with severe pain around his gall bladder. The pain would subside after a while if he lay on his right side, but sometimes the pains would come back and persist, accompanied by a fever. His diagnosis was an inflammation in the bile duct and around the liver. Åke described his general health in a way which only suggested a possible disease developing:

"Born in 1902. Height 181 cm. Hereditarily powerful constitution. Ever since my young days I have worked very hard, and later on I have worked in industrial, economic and political situations. I have always been careful to keep my body in generally good shape. All my life I have practiced some form of sport, and lately it has been mostly riding."

"I have had a tendency to overwork, but otherwise, my ways of life have been rather cautious, especially when concerning my food and beverage habits, which have been necessary from the start on account of my demands at work. My weight during the past decades has been about 75 kilograms, or 165 pounds. When my health was at its worst, my weight dropped to 66 kilograms, or about 145 pounds."

His health problems were not unique in the Wiberg family. Åke's brother Magnus suffered from the same symptoms before he had a gall bladder operation to remove a large number of gallstones. The problems persisted for Åke during the late 1930's, but they did not call for a surgical solution. His condition improved in the early 1940's and his pain attacks were less common, but things got worse in the latter part of the decade. His cholesterol levels increased and his pains came more frequently. His body reacted strongly to certain foods, specifically fatty ones, as well as strong spices. In spite of this, Åke described his general health as good, even if long trips and a heavy work load could worsen his condition.

By the end of the 1940's it was clear that his disease was getting more serious. Doctors that Åke consulted could not identify why he was sick, and several times they issued incorrect diagnoses. The lack of proper diagnoses on his health situation seriously affected his life.

His health woes in 1948 led to long periods of serious illness, and in 1949 he had to resign his commission in the Swedish Parliament. Back in 1947 his health forced him to leave the Malmö city council, and now when he had to leave his work in parliament it became clear that his time devoted to Swedish politics was at an end. This meant that Åke had to abandon the career he'd had in his sights ever since he was a student in Lund.

New doctors identified his sickness as viral hepatitis, although Åke did not feel that he had that disease. Åke's stressful life style with business management duties, his political work and engagements in corporate boards and official committees, were seen by the doctors as central to his health problems. Still lacking a clear diagnosis, they recommended he take a year off from everything and just rest up. So, the family decided to move to California for the foreseeable future. This would afford Åke ample opportunities for recreation, and he would be able to fully analyze his illness and get to know which possibilities for recovery there were "over there."

In November of 1950 the Wiberg family, two adults and three children (the youngest was nine years old) boarded a Johnson Line freighter in Gothenburg, heading for California via the Panama Canal. During their stay in Santa Barbara, Åke became better acquainted with his illness. He began to `experiment` with different medicines and maintained a journal about how his health changed and what effects the various medicines had. In the late 1950's these journal entries were collected in a medical review, "Differentiated Diagnostic Factors in One Case" which was intended for Åke's personal doctor friends. Not all of them appreciated this, as they saw the book as critical of the doctors' inability to properly diagnose an unusual disease. But this was not the author's intent at all.

Åke Wiberg remained in the USA for almost a year. His health did not improve substantially from all the relaxation he was prescribed, and the American doctors he consulted had no solution for his problems. The most trying part of this stay abroad was the devastating separation from his wife Märta in the summer of 1951. This was no agreeable, friendly divorce. They argued viciously and often, which had a terrible influence on the children, who were forced to take sides with one of their parents. Eldest son Anders supported his Dad, while the younger siblings Ann and Jan sided with their Mom.

After these incidents, Åke chose to immediately return to Sweden. Anders came on New Year's 1952 to begin studies at Lundsberg's Skola boarding school, which was located close to Apertin, where Åke spent most of his time after returning home to Sweden. Upon his return, Åke reconnected with his Swedish doctors. In early 1953, when his symptoms resembled those of cirrhosis of the liver, this fact was incorrectly combined with an earlier viral hepatitis diagnosis. Doctors would later realize that the cirrhosis had other origins. His condition got progressively worse during 1953 with continual inflammatory symptoms in his liver and gall bladder. In spite of the real dangers involved, they decided to operate on the gall bladder on May 29, 1953. This relieved the acute inflammation and meant that certain types of diseases could be ruled out. For the rest of 1953, Åke was in convalescence, which should have allowed him to improve his health. But, instead, his liver function continued to weaken.

In early 1954 he decided to move back to Stockholm and reside in his apartment on Strandvägen. Rather soon thereafter, he suffered new inflammatory attacks, and at the beginning of March he was hospitalized. Doctors had envisioned a two-week-long observation period, but it developed into a half-year's stay, new liver problems, blood clots, edema in his legs, kidney stones and abscesses in his eyes and ears. In August of 1954, his condition was such that doctors gave him only two or three weeks to live. A similar judgment, although not quite as pessimistic, was made by an international specialist: A very experienced and internationally renowned specialist, Sir Harold Hinsworth reacted to research concerning Åke's morphological changes - as well as an incorrect case history and dire prognosis. "The prognosis, whatever the man's present condition, is bad. I would be surprised if he lived as much as two years."

If his health would benefit from - or suffer from - leaving the hospital was impossible to predict. But for Åke Wiberg the times in hospitals were physically and mentally debilitating. After the doctors' latest opinions, he decided to leave the hospital as soon as possible. He arranged his own transfer by ambulance to Apertin. Before leaving he received written instructions concerning his medications:

"...including intramuscular injections certain days of B12 at a dosage of 50 micrograms. The day after my arrival at my own property I was more tired than one could imagine. I had to inject the vitamins myself. I had a number of B12 vials, whose labels of contents read 2.500 micrograms. I had a vague recollection of 50 something, but I could not believe that it was correct. Pulling up only 50 mg from a little vial containing 2.500 mg into a syringe is hardly possible even for someone very used to doing it. I seemed to remember that the dosage was 1.250, or half a vial, injected every day, and this seemed natural to me. This may seem strange to people who have never experienced liver problems, but I never even bothered to look at the label on the vial. After only a few days of these injections I began to feel much better, and my improvement continued. Naturally I had no idea if this had anything to do with the B12 vitamin doses."

Åke Wiberg had received earlier vitamin treatments, but not of B12, to alleviate shortages which arose because of his sickness. During his half year in the hospital, powerful dosages of cortisone had contributed to lessening his body's ability to process nourishment, and this continued until Åke increased his intake of B12. Åke Wiberg's own supervising physician confirmed this fact after a visit to Apertin. If he tried to discontinue his medication, his liver function and general condition would worsen. In the fall of 1954 Åke continued his increased intake of vitamin B12, and also tested increased doses of other vitamins, and of calcium. His liver functions improved gradually.

He continued his self-diagnoses during 1955 and 1956. He collected a large variety of international medical journals on liver and gall illness, and his conviction that viral hepatitis was not responsible for the symptoms of his illness grew steadily. He was finally granted access to journals maintained by previous doctors, after having been refused this access before, and he analyzed the data on the history of his illness.

Since he was not yet totally symptom-free, but only feeling better thanks to increased nutrients and improved diet, he felt it important to trace the basic origins of his sickness. This work took him to his own diagnosis that he was suffering from "an intermittent partial blockage in the [colon]," which caused a bilious cirrhosis, or repeated blockages in the bile ducts which led to the development of illness in the liver. This could be the explanation for abrupt changes in general health and liver functions, including jaundice symptoms and a swollen liver.

To verify this prognosis, upon an initiative of Åke himself, an analysis of three bile and kidney tests was undertaken in the spring of 1956. They supported the assumption concerning bile duct blockages, and on June

12, 1956 a new operation was done on the bile ducts. After a week in the hospital Åke Wiberg had not only recovered from the operation, but he felt stronger and more alert than he had in a long time.

"As I was leaving the hospital I could sense that I felt healthier than I was before. It is indeed significant that I went out into the city straight from the hospital and spent several hours at art exhibitions and in antiques stores, without feeling the least bit tired."

Åke Wiberg, with determination and self-assuredness, not only had identified his own sick state but had engineered the treatment which, through his special insight, seemed necessary. He discovered that the symptoms he had suffered through were somewhat different than those which usually appeared. Medical literature said that 90% of the cases were diagnosed via clinical observation and laboratory analysis. Unfortunately, Åke Wiberg's symptoms fell into the other 10%. This had not only resulted in a period of sickness twenty years in length, but also having to abandon a political career.

ACTIVE TO THE VERY END

His long period of poor health and sickness made Åke Wiberg most aware of his own mortality. He left his political life behind, but was still the owner and chief strategist in his diversified company group.

Compared with the hectic life he led in the 1930's and 1940's, he had a much greater opportunity in the 1950's to pursue his own personal cultural interests. He spent most of his time in the 1950's and early 1960's at Apertin, at Strandvägen 55 in Stockholm, and at Attavara during the summers. He very seldom visited the Malmö Strumpfabrik during these years. Instead he devoted a great deal of his time to managing his financial assets and holdings, where he developed his knowledge of the Swedish stock market.

A major event in Wiberg's life took place in 1955, when he married Märtha Jegerhjelm. They had known one another since the 1930's, when she was married to Ernst Wahlquist, one of the founders of Malmö Strumpfabrik. The marriage was rather unexpected, even for his son Anders. In any case the union appears to have been harmonious between the stubborn and driven Åke Wiberg and the much more relaxed Märtha Jegerhjelm.

Märtha had two children from her marriage to Ernst Wahlquist, Marianne and Staffan. It was a given for

Åke Wiberg that he would take care of them. Prominent financier Jacob Wallenberg had been a close friend of the Wahlquist family. Even after Ernst Wahlquist's death Jacob seems to have maintained very close ties with the family, and especially with Märtha Jegerhjelm. After their marriage Åke Wiberg writes in a letter to Jacob Wallenberg:

"Märtha and I and our youngsters really enjoy life together. I know I need not praise Märtha too much, as I am certain that you would agree wholeheartedly with my superlatives. I had no idea one could switch down to such a low gear and be so at home in the country.

Now that my health is back in order, we will be residing more frequently in our Stockholm apartment...You have always been a solid friend for Märtha, Staffan and Marianne - not to mention the word idol. I have also been very aware of what you, in so many ways, and for so many years, have meant to their family."

During the 1950's Apertin was often a meeting ground for Swedish cultural personalities. Its relaxed atmosphere attracted well known artists, such as Otto Sköld. Apertin also became the primary home for Åke Wiberg's expanding art collection. His initial interest had been art from the 1600's and 1700's, but his work with the Swedish Art Council exposed him to modern Swedish art. Thus, he learned a lot about, and also came to appreciate, more contemporary art.

A great deal of Åke Wiberg's work during the 1950's involved organizing and managing the considerable wealth which had been built up by his companies. His last five or six years he relaxed by dictating his memories of family and places he enjoyed, and he published them in book form in 1959. This was a way Åke could relay his own family history to coming Wiberg generations.

A typical work day for Åke Wiberg began at exactly 9 a.m. with his arrival at the office. By then the mail had been opened, sorted and distributed by office personnel. Wiberg preferred letter writing to talking on the phone, and this led to a large number of incoming letters.

While he went through his mail, company lawyer and colleague Göran Mörner stood near Åke's desk and jotted down his comments. At 9.30 this work was done, and he took an hour's walk around Djurgården Park nearby.

Åke Wiberg employed three secretaries for a long time. Once back from his morning constitutional, he dictated letters to his first secretary, primarily concerning business matters and answers to incoming letters. He expected that this morning correspondence would be written out and ready for signing in the afternoon. After lunch, which was from noon to 1 p.m., he dictated to his second secretary, business correspondence and lighter chronicles concerning family history – he published four books in 1959 alone.

The second secretary's notes had to be typed out by lunch the following day. After a short coffee break Åke dictated to his third secretary. His work day was completed at 6 p.m., when he took the elevator up to his apartment off the same stairway. This work schedule was adhered to Monday through Saturday, and if his Sunday was also calm he would work on Sunday afternoon as well.

Åke Wiberg, alongside a large number of businessmen of his time, held a strong aversion for the Swedish tax system. The increased tax burdens after WWII were also a hot political issue, especially for the right-wing party. Åke Wiberg saw capital management within his own foundation and in Borgen Management AB as ways to reduce his tax payments. He could also reduce his taxes via internal transactions between his companies. His actions in these business and legal areas were closely monitored by the Swedish tax authorities more than one time.

Åke Wiberg suffered a major setback in the fall of 1963 when the press revealed that he was accused of tax evasion. The problems were from an errant corporate tax revision in February 1962, problems which Åke and his colleagues were well aware of. The first tax inquiry released in November 1963 indicated that a series of fraudulent transactions in 1959 and 1960 were carried out in an attempt to exempt about six million kronor from taxation. Åke Wiberg insisted all the while that these transactions were fully legal.

The newspapers made this a headline item, and on November 19, 1963 *Expressen* described the situation as follows:

"A Malmö company in the same concern sold a shipment of goods for SEK [Swedish Kronor] 28,000 to a partner company. Then this firm sold the same goods to the corporate foundation, which then sold these goods to a third partner company in the concern, which sold them back to the original company in Malmö. The price tag by then was exactly SEK 1,476,347."

A final verdict was never reached in this tax case. Six days after this tax evasion case was publicized through the press, Åke Wiberg died, and the court felt that it would be very difficult to gain clarity in how these internal transactions were organized, as Åke Wiberg had been the one who directed them.

The tax process involved Åke Wiberg as a person, which was confirmed by the fact that the federal prosecutor placed an injunction on any distribution of some of his personal assets and property. No other serious problems were to result from this intervention by the tax authorities. The media's presentation of the situation appears to have been somewhat overdramatized. No legal punishment nor criminal responsibility was mentioned, and the taxation penalties were significantly more moderate than what the press had expected. They were paid in full without protest.

Åke Wiberg's improved health after his gall bladder operation was very short-lived. But the greatest threat to his long-term recovery was not his liver problems. He suffered badly from respiratory and throat problems in the summer of 1963, and was admitted for a thorough checkup at Lund Hospital. The doctors quickly realized that he had advanced lung cancer and that he needed immediate surgery. Even if the surgery worked, his prognosis for lengthy survival was poor.

The operation removed a part of one of his lungs, but his general condition was unsatisfactory and he suffered serious morning pains. He often felt better in the afternoon and evening, primarily when he had the company of his closest colleagues, Anders Wiberg and Göran Mörner.

Åke Wiberg was under severe pressure when the demands from Swedish tax authorities became known. On the morning of November 25, 1963, he took his rifle and his dog out into the Apertin woods to hunt foxes, and he would never return from this hunting trip. News of his death and his coming tax evasion trial drowned in the deluge of news following President John F. Kennedy's murder, which happened three days earlier.

LEGACY

During his lifetime Åke Wiberg built up an impressive fortune, primarily thanks to Malmö Strumpfabrik. He had already transferred some of his wealth in the 1950's to the Åke Wiberg Foundation for scientific research, but after his death, he left very valuable assets to be distributed according to his will to a number of beneficiaries, both within and outside of the family.

An estate inventory can provide a good idea of someone's personality and views on life. It shows not only which assets and debts one leaves behind, but also how organized he or she was, and if he or she lived frugally or was an avid collector. The estate inventory can also reveal which interests in general the person had. The combination of all these things contributes to our understanding of the person in question, and in the case of Åke Wiberg's estate inventory we are given a lot of information.

Åke Wiberg left three complementary wills, to eliminate any grounds for disagreements amongst beneficiaries after his death. Two wills clarified who would be appointed estate administrators and executors of the wills. The third will, dated November 18, 1963 establishes how the assets are to be distributed amongst beneficiaries and how the process will be handled. The guidelines Åke drew up were quite closely adhered to. The largest portion of the assets went to his wife, Märtha Wiberg, and the three children, while various capital insurances and funds went to more distant relatives, earlier colleagues and good friends.

The estate inventory was, for its time, very comprehensive. The list filled 130 pages, and included the Apertin estate, the apartment at Strandvägen 55, Åke's office in the same building, and finally Banergatan 4 in Stockholm, where the corporate wood companies were headquartered. His art collections were so comprehensive that specialists had to be called in to evaluate them.

Most of the art Åke Wiberg collected over the years was located on the Apertin estate and at Strandvägen 55. Exhibits included oil paintings and watercolors of older masters such as Rubens, Tintoretto, van Dyck and Gauguin, as well as contemporary Swedish artists. Collections also included antique items and folk-art pieces from different lands and eras, such as groups of East Indian porcelain and Japanese and Chinese art objects. His more unique collections were: about two hundred Swedish and foreign pocket watches; eighty religious icons from the Mediterranean and Russia; a hundred or so flint axes and a large number of bronze mortars.

These interests portray not only a wealthy man, but a person with a well-developed taste for art and creative collecting. During the last fifteen to twenty years of his life, art was his true goal in life, and his commercial operations were his way of reaching that goal.

PHOTOS AND CAPTIONS

Åke Wiberg acquired Apertin Manor in Värmland in 1939. The estate became a central point for him and his family, as well as for Åke's contacts with politicians and cultural figures. It also figures prominently in his first wife, Dr. Marta Holmström's oral history and memoirs.

Swedish King Gustaf VI Adolf visits Apertin Manor and admires Åke Wiberg's collection of pocket watches

Åke Wiberg (civilian clothes) together with Swedish soldiers who were quartered at Apertin Manor during World War II.

NOTE by ETW: As for Malmö Strumpfabrik, it originally moved from Copenhagen to Torggatan 20 C in Malmö in 1926. Then in 1929 they moved to Trelleborgsvägen. That avenue connects the southern city of Trelleborg with the road connecting Malmö with Copenhagen. In 2007 on a New York City subway I overheard young Swedes and introduced myself. The said their grandfather had worked for MSF and that it was now a mixed-use mall and residential complex. Then I had to disembark.

The Malmö State Archive has a great deal of information: malmo.se/Kultur--fritid/Kultur--noje/Arkiv--historia/Kulturarv-Malmo/P-S/Strumpfabriken.html

Swedish Wikipedia does also:
sv.wikipedia.org/wiki/Malm%C3%B6_Strumpfabrik

The family grave where Åke Wiberg and his second wife, Märtha(Jegerhjelm, Wahlquist) Wiberg, rest on the island of Djurgården, central Stockholm, Sweden. It is a special, very peaceful place, mostly surrounded by water, and traditionally a naval officer's resting place. Immediately beyond the stone wall are the memorial to the *Estonia* ferry sinking victims (which two distant Wachtmeister relatives, a brother and sister, managed to survive), and the museum for the royal ship *Vasa*, sunk in 1628.

Although his second wife and her daughter are buried together, and his step-son Steffan Wahlquist and his father are also buried not far away, none of Åke Wiberg' direct descendants are buried there. It was his preferred walking destination each morning after opening mail in his home office nearby. His first wifeMärta is buried across Stockholm, at the Engelbrekt Church, at Östermalmsgatan 20, down the road from her longtime apartment and near her daughter Ann's primary residence.

PART III

INTERVIEW WITH DR. MÄRTA (HOLMSTRÖM)
WIBERG
BY ERIC TROELS WIBERG, STOCKHOLM, 28
MARCH, 1992

MÄRTA WIBERG

Farmor, interviewed in conversation and recorded by pen, Karlavägen 50, Östermalm.

At her kitchen table of her flat and doctor's office, where she lived alone from about 1953 to the summer of 1999, when she passed about 94 years of age. I was a twenty-one-year-old student at Oxford on my way to a three-week solo backpacking trip through East Africa.

This is not for genealogical, but rather for human interest and story-telling interest. There is no necessary order, it was a free-flowing conversation. One of my focusses was on discovering what properties and farms were where, and who owned what, and what was connected to Åke and her and what wasn't, as it was all confusing to me up to that point.

She was born in Malmö in 1905. Her Morfar, or mother's father, had a law degree, or LLB. All of her family came from Malmö and Värmland, or southern Sweden. Her children Anders and Ann (my dad and aunt) met their grandmother Maria when she was aged 87.

He grandfather's family, the Holmströms, had a "big" factory in Malmö, with six or seven employees. They made wagons, or the centers of wagons. The family were in the business of manufacturing wagons which were sold under the name or brand *Gajee* or similar. In the Malmö area about 1900. Märta's father's sister said that the family lived on one side of a courtyard and that the employees lived on the other, and that they all ate together. This was circa 1850's. The factory location is occupied by a large theater.

One of her aunts became a masseuse Germany and/or France, and did not marry. Her father Dr. Johan Holmström died of cancer about age 81. Her mother Irma was about twelve years younger. She lived until age 84. Märta's son Anders [my Dad] met his Mormor Irma. Apparently, she washed her grandson at Attavara, the farm which Åke had bought to keep the family safe in WWII. After his Mormor washed Anders fully, he rather precociously asked her, "are you not shy to look at a naked man?" He was about four or five years old at the time......!

NOTE: My parents both firmly agree that Dr. Johan and Irma divorced, and that would explain why Dad was told that though he never "met" his grandfather, Dr. Holmström would sit in the same park Anders was playing in to see his grandson. Apparently, it was not an amicable divorce. No reason for it is given, however later oral history suggests he may have been a workaholic and placed the family third behind the clinic and his sailing – see Feb. 12, 1999 oral history.

Farmor had four sisters, one became an eye doctor like their father, Farmor became a general practitioner doctor who worked on at least one Swedish Prime Minister, and Maya, whose grandson Niclas stayed with the family in Bahamas and whose son Lars taught Eric and John to sail in Sweden. Another sister, known as "Mi" died suddenly in Malmö in 1941.

Mi's daughter died at birth/stillborn. There are sad notes but specific, like "several common law husbands," and "childbirth – died stillborn," so there was clearly some tragedy in MI's life.

Inga apparently suffered Scarlet Fever as a child, and it affected her brain. She was believed by Farmor to still be alive in 1992. She was hospitalized in Gothenburg for the Scarlet Fever. It says she died in 1990. She liked to do handiwork (needlework, knitting, crafts) and lived in Lidingö outside Stockholm, but the funeral was in Malmö.

Farmor was clearly not fond of her sister Maya, writing "quarreled with Lars and Farmor," and "eccentric," and "crazy on money." In conclusion, she said that "all married," with Mi apparently having one or more common law husbands.

Farmor was born in June of 1905. Her middle name is Siri. She went top private school for girls at *Bunthskolan* – non-religious. Age nineteen she took the exams, matriculated [from Gymnasium or similar, high-school-like educations] and attended Lund University outside Malmö from 1924. To age twenty-one, when took the *studentenexamen* and passed, she was then able to formally attend Lund full time.

Between 1925 and 1934 studied in Lund. Married 2.5 years into her exam studies. Åke was an advokat / solicitor, not an "attorney" by definition. Göran Mörner is a "lawyer" – a solicitor is like a "public lawyer" – she said that Grandmommy, Jane's father Ralph McDermid, was an Attorney / Advokat."

NOTE: The distinction appears to lie in whether one goes to court or not.

Åke and Märta met at a wedding c.1928, and married in 1931.Åke was born 30 March 1902, a day before Ann [Ann Dillon Wachtmeister, my sister's birthday] on 31 March. WWII came 1939-1945, and the family spent much time at Apertin. Lived there, it was their base.

In 1941 both of her in-laws - Åke's parents- died the same year – his mother in May, and his and Magnus' father in August, and Troels/Truls died in December 1941, one week before.

Malevik is a village on an island on the west coast connected by causeway to Gothenburg to the east. At one time is was a rural setting, now it is more like a suburb. One of our relatives, an officer in the army, lost a finger when the train between both locations tipped over. Åke's parents' family home. Farmor says that it was sold about

1990 by her children Ann and Jan for five to six million kronor. Magnus' relatives are believed to have held onto their property in Kullavik or Malevik for longer, including a daughter who married a Belizean.

NOTE: Mom and Dad say that only Åke's siblings – like Margot and Magnus, inherited or bought properties at Malevik, not Åke himself. Also, they have no record of Ann and Jan selling.

Attavara is a farm in rural Sweden. Åke and Farmor bought this farm together in 1937-1938. It is near Halmstad, about 180 (US) miles north of Malmö, near Småland.

Apertin is a large elegant country estate built to host kings on their long journeys between Stockholm, Oslo and other places. It was purchased by Åke and Farmor in 1939 and sold in 1964 or so following Åke's death. Several of Åke's grandchildren have been there. Farmor worked extremely hard to restore it and was recognized for this by large illustrated articles in Swedish magazines. She was very proud of it (and upset when Apertin was moved into by Åke's second wife).

Farmor's son Anders has fond memories of Apertin. Originally designed as a safe place in WWII, it was later where Åke would rest and recuperate from ill health and get away from his strenuous business and political career. There are many photos in family albums of Åke riding horses and reclining in chairs in the sun at Apertin, smiling.

Misterhult belonged to Elsa (formerly Johnsson) and her husband Magnus Wiberg, and passed to their daughters Margaretta Oleinikoff and Kjerstin von Essen.

Magnus is Åke's brother (the financial officer of Malmö Stumpfabrik). Magnus's nickname was "Masse."

NOTE: *Bahama Wibergs* visited Misterhult about 1980 and were able to meet "Aunt Elsa," cut hay and swam in lakes. Eric got lost on a bike. We learned German harvest songs.

Åke's older sister Margot was a dentist. He had another sister named Cajsa or similar. Farmor said she has a son named Jan and that she married a man named Diehl

NOTE: Eric found a Dr. Jan Thorsen Diehl, born 1932, who has been a radiologist in Dallas Texas for many years, called and left a message in Dec. 2017 - he is 85 now.

Farmor's sisters had children – Bibi has a girl and two boys who a pharmacist, a doctor, and teacher. As we know, Mi's daughter died at a young age. Maya's only child was Lars, the Army Colonel sailor, who died around 1995. He and his wife had Niclas and a daughter.

From her siblings' offspring, seven survived birth and six may still have been alive in 1992. Add Farmor's three children, and Dr. Johan and Irma had ten living grand-children and probably over twenty great-grandchildren.

Her family of five moved for just over a year to Santa Barbara California Sept. 1950-1952. Later on, she notes the move to California was to "save the marriage." Then in 1952 divorce, and she moved out (presumably from the waterfront buildings Åke owned on Strandvägen, at 55, or Fredrikshovsgatan). Then Åkepurchased the apartment at Karlavägen 50 for Farmor to live in. It is on the same island, and still a very posh neighborhood.

INTERVIEW WITH MRS. GUNNEL (HELGOSDOTTER WIBERG) LINDROTH BY ERIC WIBERG, BAHAMAS, 12 APRIL, 2011

GUNNEL HELGOSDOTTER WIBERG

Introduction:

This was a roughly two-hour interview at Gunnel Lindroth's apartment at Cable Beach Manor. We recorded the entire conversation, and I also wrote rough notes. We consulted the Wiberg branch family tree history book, *Bjära Släkten*, in two volumes. The interview was "on deadline," – it began at 11:45, as my wife Alex was packing our luggage at the house, and we had a 4 p.m. flight to New York to catch! It was many years before I found the recording and transcribed it. I have skipped over difficult and awkward passages trying to establish family genealogy – all of that information is readily available in the family book as well as the extraordinary family tree created by her son Magnus Lindroth of Switzerland, on Ancestry.com.

My main motivation was to capture the compelling human-interest story of this amazing woman, in her 90's, whose son Orjan I had come to know, to ask her what it was like to greet my father Anders Wiberg when he arrived in the Bahamas first in 1959 then "forever" in the mid 1960's. Another goal was to place her brother Orjan, who I stayed with on a farm in Vänersborgin the late 1980s with his two adopted children in perspective.

The overriding goal is to explain who the original Bahama Wibergs came to be, and she and her husband and sons are a primary reason. Information not directly relating to her development as a Wiberg and with Arne leading up to their life in the Bahamas are largely skimmed or passed over.

She was born Gunnel Wiberg in May 1922, the oldest of two brothers; Alan and Orjan. Her little sister died at five months old. When the little girl died, her mother blamed herself. Apparently, she caught a terrible cold. Gunnel says she wishes she didn't experience that at age three. They lived and were born around Helgo near Stockholm – this probably explains her name Helgosdotter. At first, her father worked as the Post Master, then he became a writer for the peace or anti-war movement in the wake of World War I. He was the co-founder of a group outside Stockholm like a Swedish United Nations-type of group. An Alliance for Peace or to protect from war. She thinks it was called the Swedish Peace and Freedom Forum.

Her mother was from Vänersborg, west Sweden. She studied Art at Wilhelmsen's Art School in Gothenburg. A talented painter. Thinks she would have met with acclaim. Orjan [Gunnel's son] has one of the watercolors. Her brother Allan was a gentleman farmer, but was felled by smoking three to four packets of cigarettes a day. Small farm, cows, forests. Their brother Orjan was interested by his travels to India and adapted two children from there, a boy and a girl, not siblings. Their names are Alan and Karin, after Orjan's wife's sister. Her Farfar, or father's father, was Martin, born 1826 – Helgo's father - a mathematical genius. Died 1880 in Viby, Skåne.

How Gunnel met her husband, Arne:

By 1940 the Nazis had occupied Norway and Denmark, and there was fighting in Finland too, so Sweden was quite surrounded by the war. Gunnel volunteered at age eighteen years and was [to her amazement] issued with a Mauser pistol and a uniform and sent to man a high watchtower in Lapland near the Norwegian border in the summer. Her job was to listen for planes and radio them in when she heard them [she heard plenty, did not actually see one!] She went on from May to August, 1940, before the bitter northern winter set in.

Her call sign was *66845 ODAM* she never wrote it down, and never forgot it. During that time, in the nearby community, she met Arne. He was a pilot of a small plane and had a license to shoot down German planes. One Sunday she went to the store to buy a birthday present for a friend from Nyköping. [She said something about she studied seven years of German and sang *"ichhabeneinmehr"* or, *I want no more*?) about homesickness which I don't fully understand].

Gunnel was not "interested" in Arne because he was 13 years older than her – he was 31, she was 18. Arne was born December 9, 1908, and died in Stockholm in 1979. They were married in 1945, March 3, also in Stockholm, at a time when making any kind of celebration of such things as weddings was "not done." For the wedding, they went to the manse where the priest lived near Nyköping. Her grandparents and parents came. Spånga was one of the oldest towns in Sweden – about 1100 AD. Swedes were expected to give their meagre funds to their neighbors the Finns, not spend on a wedding.

Arne was an only child. Arne's father was from an island in the archipelago near Norrtälje, and built boats near Nyköping possibly called Nyköping Boat Works. Very good with boats. May have been Lindroth Boatbuilding. His mother came to the wedding but his father died of pneumonia early in the 1930s and could not. Gunnel and Arne had a courtship via mail. He booked seats for them at a theater on New Years' 1940-1941. First, she said "Yes," then last minute "No" and later learned he had been the very first one to buy the tickets to the show. She was age 22 in 1945 five years later at a Lutheran church.

Arne got a job with ABA Airlines (AB Aero transport, one quarter of SAS, or Scandinavian Air Services. They moved to Norrtälje because of an opportunity to work with Axel Wenner-Gren, a wildly successful industrialist who had a financial interest in ABA. Wenner-Gren had a light train factory and Arne worked there for two years up to 1952. The two met through Arne working out how many trains would be needed. SAS started in 1946 special *(railspus?)* train – was made for smaller tracks, lived in Spånga still. In order to buy their first house, they took a modest loan from the government, as was common in all Scandinavian countries at the time.

Moving to the Bahamas, 1952:

Gunnel took the two boys, ages two and seven, and they all flew "National" airlines. Re-fueled in Gander Newfoundland, the US military air base closer to European air fields. Then direct to Nassau. Arne was waiting at the landing strip (Anders believes this may have been Windsor Field, now the site of the National Stadium, though in the mid-1950s the main airfield moved to its present location). They had an apartment rented at "Hog Cay" which became "Paradise Island."

Wenner-Gren – their employer, was at first based on his estate called Shangri-La, on Paradise Island, but then Huntington Hartford bought it and they pulled out in a few months to Eastern Road. The Lindroths found an extraordinary lattice-work home colonial style several floors at West Street Downtown Nassau (then a ridge occupied by highest society, mostly neglected now, near Graycliff Hotel). It was for sale, and they bought it.

Arne had a car as well as a driver. It was a US – built car. He ran a private bank. They did not lend money, they borrowed it. Arne had obtained a degree in finance at Stockholm's Handels Skola. They had heard of Anders Wiberg (Dad) because Anders' father Åke had written to them in Bahamas to say, in essence "I have a son who doesn't know where to settle, and may be interested in the Bahamas." She said Anders was "blonde, blue-eyed, a little overweight, very great personality."

Gunnel said that one day, Anders said to me [Dad was about 15 years younger than Gunnel] "I have met a girl on the beach," and Gunnel said to herself, "Oh no, here we go"! Then she met the young lady [and it was Mom, Jane – so the story goes] and when she saw how lovely and charming Jane was, she was very relieved and happy. She was "charming and pleasant."

Explaining how Åke knew her family, she said her "father cooperated with, and coauthored the book with Åke," meaning *Bjära Släkten*. Gunnel says she met a Swedish lady on the beach at PI who ended up asking Gunnel a lot of prying questions about how Åke placed his money, and it made Gunnel distrust this woman a lot and distance herself from her. She things the woman may have had "some kind of title." Marguerite, the wife of Axel Wenner-Gren, left Baltimore on a ship to return to Europe. Was going to sing in Austria after the war.

Arne was in charge of everything for Wenner-Gren in Bahamas – vice president, Bank of the Bahamas. Arne wanted to be involved with a new kind of computer. A smart man from California talked him into it. Took whole ball room for a presentation in 1968. Wishing to form a joint venture, but the bank was bleeding money. Wenner-Gren wanted to harvest gold and minerals in British Columbia Canada (Gunnel thought out loud: if it was so easy why haven't the locals done it?).

They then travelled for one year – Nyköping, Stockholm– and felt welcomed back all over. They also felt it was time to leave Wenner-Gren. Sold Shangri-La after about eight years, 1959-1970. Had to vacate in about four to six weeks. Wenner-Gren died in about 1968. The ships he and Marguerite travelled back to Europe on tended to be the Swedish America Line liners *Grippsholm* and *Kungsholm*. Arne had surgery on a hernia at, thought to be esophageal, or dealing with the passage between the throat and the stomach. He died at the hospital outside Stockholm and was buried not far aware from there.

"Your father Anders has done everything on his own. Arne respected Anders very much."

Extracts from the actual recording:

Arne was trained in finance in Stockholm, where he got a degree. His father worked on work boats - many boats. Apparently, he was very good at it. She knew of Anders because Åke had written and said, "I have a son who is going to ... He doesn't know where to settle down and he might be interested in Bahamas." So, Anders came. She was very happy that he was able to visit from South America. She thinks that Anders was about twenty-four years old at the time [Dad is born 1935, so yes, in 1959 he was twenty-four]. She said "he was very good-looking. He was blonde and blue-eyed, though he was a little overweight. But he had a very direct personality and very charming, funny, and likeable."

Gunnel says that one day, Anders "...came to me and he said, "I have met a girl on the beach." I thought, "God help us," because I knew what that was. I thought, "Well, poor Anders." But then Jane came in and I saw it was completely different. Not one of those girls they pick up from beaches."

NOTE: She was not at the party with the Ronnie and Joan Carrols the night that Anders met Jane, which was later, after they left, about December 1964, as Mom and Dad married in Spring 1966. The Swedish Santa Lucia party.

Gunnel said she knows Farmor Märta better than she knew Åke, who was older.

She said she met Åke and that "...he was very handsome. I think you and Anders look like him." [blush!]She said that he was pleasant and charming. ".... of course, that he met someone else, that is normal, too, you know." She feels she met him about 1944. She said that her father had had lots of contact with him through this book, which is the family history book which Åke oversaw.

That's how Åke got her and Arne's address in Bahamas to write to them and say Anders was coming to visit the Bahamas. Gunnel added that "then later on I remember ... I can't remember when, but I met this Swedish lady on Paradise Beach and she knew Åke and Märta[our Farmor, not his second wife]. I understand that she wanted to find out all of the details because she had heard that they were separated. She didn't know anything from me. Not a word. She was gold-digging – or rumor-mongering."

She spoke briefly about Marguerite Wenner-Gren, saying she was from Baltimore and left United States on board a ship to go to Europe, probably Germany or Austria, to sing after World War I. She had an apparently fairly good or above average voice. And that's how she met Axel Wenner-Gren. She must have been seventeen and he was twenty-seven and they got married apparently right away. She didn't dare to tell her parents until about year later. She thinks they were married in Paris. When Gunnel met the Wenner-Grens, they were at the top, but the decline started later. She said they had about ten executives working for them in the Bahamas. Arne was in charge of everything. They borrowed money, not lent it.

Gunnel says that "It was absolutely right away my husband knew that it [the bank] could never go well the way they did it. He wanted to be involved with this, the new kind of computers. He had a very smart man from Gothenburg, no, from California who talked him into that. Then Westinghouse wanted to get with Wenner-Gren, but he said, "Absolutely not, I don't need anybody." She goes on about another scheme to harvest minerals and gold from British Columbia, Canada, but Gunnel thought – if it was such an easy brilliant way to profit, why haven't the locals done it?

Gunnel and Arne travelled from Bahamas to Sweden each year, to Linköping and Stockholm. They also returned for Arne's mother funeral. At first, they would take ships, but later they would fly. From New York they took ships named the *Kungsholm* and *Grippsholm*– believed to be part of the Swedish-American Line. "That was lots of fun, but it took too much time. Arne probably had four, six weeks off each year. It was when he was always in Stockholm then. When I asked if "it quite prestigious to be married to Arne? He was quite an important man in town?" she replied "I never felt like that, but I guess so."

When I asked if the other ladies were polite to her, and very considerate of her and if she felt welcomed in Nassau, she replied: "Yes, but I never thought of prestige." She lived in Nassau from 1952 to 1970. The left "because we thought it was time to leave." She makes a business-related statement about nobody is able to make a profit with a 25% interest to pay on the money they borrowed. Also, some reference to staying on after Wenner-Gren and working for Huntington Hartford.

In 1970 they "....went to Spain for a little while, and Arne did some business there, in Malaga, where there were many Swedes." The children did not join them as they were studying in London School of Economics (Orjan), London University (Magnus), Edinburgh (Ulf) and Sweden (Lizzie).

I asked if she and Arne encouraged Dad (Anders) to settle in Bahamas, and help him find the Cable Beach Manor. She replied that "....we had nothing to do with. He had done absolutely whatever he wanted. Anders did this all by himself." [Since we were sitting in Cable Beach Manor, which Dad bought in the mid-60s and he and Mom have run since, she obviously means his and their investments and accomplishments and family since].

"The Manor and all..." I ask. "Yes," she replies. I then ask "Did Arne respect Anders?" to which she replied: "Very much. We all did. I loved him. I wish that Anders was here sometimes.

NOTE: She appears to forget that Anders was at the Manor every day... This is uncharacteristic, as in all other respects she was 100% lucid.

I made a comment about how likeable Dad is, to which she replied, "Very. He reminds me, in his manners, of the way my father talked, you know. Disappearing away [those types of old-school manners] but he is very, very nice. I replied, "I agree. He's a wonderful man. He didn't have an easy childhood, I don't think. I don't think there was a lot of love with his father. I really love him, too." Gunnel Lindroth passed away about two years later, in her mid-nineties, in the Bahamas, roughly 60 years after she arrived there.

INTERVIEWS WITH DR. MÄRTA (HOLMSTRÖM) WIBERG BY JANE (McDERMID) WIBERG, 12 FEBRUARY, 1999, STOCKHOLM

Jane McDermid Wiberg, interviewed Farmor for her life stories and other vignettes via tape. She said Farmor would become tired and the stories thus did not go on for very long. Also in the background can be heard her son (my father, Anders) as well as her great-grandchildren Oscar and Wilhelm (Axel was only a few months old), as well as Gustaf Wachtmeister, their father. So, clearly, this was a family time. As you will see, it was also good timing. Jane helped her along, and they laughed a lot. (How the tapes went from Sweden to storage in Bahamas, then Manhattan, where they cassette player had to replaced, then the tapes broke, and they had to be broken open and re-spliced, is a story for another day....).

Recorded around 12 February, 1999, in Farmor's apartment at Karlavägen 50, Stockholm:

PART I: FAMILY, CHILDHOOD, EARLY LIFE

I will speak in English because I have go this machine from my eldest son Anders and his wife in America and she is the one who forces me to speak into it (laugh) and she is sitting at my bed drinking coffee, I am in Karlavägen. I am 93 years old, my name is Märta Siri Holmström, and I have been married Wiberg, but I am divorced. I have taken my maiden name partly because I wanted to, and partly because I am designated as a medical doctor in the name of Märta Holmström and that is the name I want to work in.

I was married to Åke for twenty years and have three children born after five to six years of marriage. That was in order to give me the opportunity to take my medical or med-list degree. Of that I am very, very, very grateful that I did, otherwise I don't know what I would have done when I divorced, because divorce I had to do.

I was born the 7th of May 1905, in Malmö, as one of five sisters, I am number four. My other sister Mi, was born 1900, Inga in 1902, then, in 1903, and I 1905 and Maya born September, 1909.

My father was medical specialist in eyes at Avagatan(street name) number 78 from 1895 - he had a private clinic for ophthalmology until he died in 1948. And as far as I know, he was almost every day, even on

Sundays, he was at work, and absolutely most precious thing in his life was his eye practice. We children and the family and the house at (street name) number five and the garden were absolutely nothing to him compared to the clinic. And I think, really, after the clinic came his boat named *Siri* (Laughs), which was down at the harbor. [Boat and her middle name are same].

He was a born sailor, and he sailed every day he could, but he did not go long sailing for weeks, since that would have taken too long time from his practice, so it was to sail to Copenhagen, Denmark, perhaps and back to Malmö. There were all those prizes, silver cups, we had on the bookshelves in the drawing room, all the way, and they were divided among the five children.

My Mama was born 1878 and was twelve years older than my father. She was a big woman, not fat, but big breasts, tall and very beautiful figure, and dressed very well, but made all the dresses herself because she did not put much money on her appearance. But she was well dressed, always – I don't know how she did it. Anyway, she always had three maids in the house, so as far as understand, she didn't do much kitchen work and all that. She was an artist – one of the best in Malmö and Sweden with embroidery, she was famous, she made a lot of things, painted plates, etc., I don't think the porcelain was very well known.

Her maiden name was Irma Muller. My grandfather was a lawyer and he had only brothers – five or six in all so far as I know. All also became lawyers except one who had a big farm. He had a house of his own in (street name) in Lund, at one of the streets.

NOTE: The next paragraphs may not make sense, a rare case where she lost her train of thought.

In the beginning it was just big fields, and I know that they had a large house, and there were two girls busy both unmarried – Lizzie was one. This was my mother's cousin, and they were quite famous, and they had a brother, that I know. But all three, the parents and the brother all were killed in an accident with horses. The horses turned around on the cart and they were killed, her parents and the brother. And they were all Mullers.

Farmor said that on both sides of her family - Holmström and Muller – they were from Malmö. All born in Malmö, a lot of brothers. Nowadays, no more Holmströms in Malmö. Just Maya and Farmor are left. There were quarrels in the family, and they didn't stay together. It is too long to go into the whole family, it was a big family living in Oskarshamn, Gothenburg, etc.

NOTE: Story of her father having one of the first cars in Malmö. Unfortunately, Farmor was feeling too tired to continue, ended after this introduction, and the topic was lost.

When we were children at Bjorkmok (neighborhood of Malmö), we were rather wild, and did a lot of things our parents had no idea about. Among other things, during the winter we jumped on the toes of the skates from one ice flake (floe, or ice pancake) out in the middle of Öresund (the strait between Denmark) with ten meters (thirty feet) beneath us, and we told no one about it. Mi -oldest sister - was eighteen, I was thirteen, something like that.

The two of us were always the wildest of the children, always doing things we were not supposed to do, and that was great fun. We never dropped into the water, and we did that often, and it was not unusual. But the winters were very hard then, and it was usual that the whole of Öresund froze in the winter, and there was no traffic, or hardly any traffic. That is absolutely unique nowadays, when we have much milder winters.

Then I remember once, when we were sitting at the window in the house, there came two children dragging a small thing that you have to pull – a kind of small sleigh with blades, yes – and with a child of maybe ten or eleven years lying on it dripping wet and it was minus ten or fifteen degrees, and she had fallen her into the sea, and they were dragging her I don't know where to.

We jumped outside and pulled her into the house, and undressed the child – which I think was a girl - and placed her into the warm water. Then we telephoned the taxi to take her to the home, to her home. If we had not done that the child would have been dead before reaching the main street. We never understood that we had saved a life, as it seemed natural to us to have done that.

Then of course when we were up around age eighteen, we took a driving license for one of the three Ford model cars, the open ones, the *73* it was named. I remember when I took my driving license, and a friend of my fathers was an engineer at a big company, and then I go out there, and then he asked me what three things are needed when driving a car, and I replied, it was "Water Benzene and Oil" and that was very good he said, and then the exam was over.

Then we had to show that I could drive, and it was out at the *fabrik* firm at the outskirts of Malmö, and we sat down, in the 73, and he was next to me, and I drove. There was not a single car in the neighborhood, and I just drove around the square. All those buildings [she is laughing heartily] and that was it and there I had my driver's license.

Very different from today, when they pay hundreds of crowns to be introduced to the heart of the city and are refused a license because of negligence. And I have never, answered one more question about driving in my whole life I have driven, since I was eighteen until age nineteen, but never once been questioned about a motor car that I could not answer. Though I don't know anything about the motor of a car, but I am a very good driver.

PART II: *EXAMEN*, LUND, MEDICAL SCHOOL

Now we come to the school time. My parents decided that I should take the Student Exam, and I had decided that I should not, so, there was first a fight. Then I said no, no, no, I intended to finish the eight classes of the girl school then take a place in a *bureau* [clerk's or administrative office], and then get married or something. But they had decided differently, and then I said "alright, but if I do, I will go in Lund, as my school comrades from Malmö, all of them will go to Lund and travel back and forth every day, it only takes twenty minutes. And after a little while, they decided that would be alright."

All the teachers I had been with at the girl's school were all laughing to learn that the Holmström girl who did the worst in the school, and could hardly spell. It was true, yet I had hidden my true value from them, and I knew very well that I could if I wanted it. There were girls from different schools – six travelled each way every day. One from *Stenkula Skola* (one of a few private girl's schools). One was Elsa Erickson, who was a star pupil from the school, and she could do everything including mathematics, and I just stole the mathematics problems and copied them from her on the train in the morning, and thanks to that I passed.

Then we were in the academy and for lunch we went with Mrs. Fisherström to a private house, Elsa, Rene,

Anna Lipta and I went there, and had breakfast every day. The train between Malmö and Lund went every hour at twenty minutes past, then we had half an hour to stroll at the platform and look at the boys strolling there, before the train started out.

After three years, to my own great astonishment, I took the student exam with rather good remarks [laughs] and nobody was more surprised than I was, because I had little marks in Swedish, but in a lot of things I had high marks, I was more surprised. Then I had made that. Then a fight started with my father on whether I should study medicine, because I didn't want that either, I wanted to start in a bureau.

Then after a little while, I took for a term a place in a private house up at Laerum outside Gothenburg with the Bement/Becker family who had a single daughter. She had a governess, and I was used only to meet doctor's people, physicians were the only ones who had any business. I packed my riding boots and helmet, and some nice dresses, that I had made myself, and I went up to this big event there.

And there I got the shock of my life. I had never been, I don't want to speak bad of those people that I had a job with, but I was one class over them, and that was that, and they looked at me as something very queer, I did things that they didn't do. I didn't ask to sit down and play piano, I just did it. Naturally. And they were surprised and not very pleasantly surprised either. That was that, it was not a great success at all. Then I went home to my home, and when I arrived in the evening one of the tutors, Stig Wiberg came down to the station to meet me [in Malmö presumably] and there was the high life, and things and normal things going on and that was that.

Now, I will begin with the medical studies, I took the *examen* in 1924, then slowly and reluctantly began studying medicine, but my father just forced me more or less. I didn't know what I wanted to do, except to sit in a bureau, but I was supposed to be intelligent, which I could not understand either, but which I apparently was, since I took my degree with very good grades.

Then, after three to four years, in I think 1929 it must have been, I took the med list (or medical candidate exams). Before that, during those courses, we were among a group of fifty, a group of four to six girls, and they were all girls from the schools – students, and they were quite nice. I lived at home in the house in Malmö, but after the med-can, all the girls, almost all the girls except two – Inga Venster, an old classmate from Malmö and I – got on with the medical exams.

And the others went to medical/dental education in Stockholm. So, we were the only two girls in the class of about fifty. Then it was more complicated with the medical education, as we dealt with the living material, and had classes, different classes – internal, surgery, pediatrics, etc. etc. That was very different, and you start with one class at 8 a.m. [she continues, but the tape has run out].

PART III: APERTIN, CAUGHT IN NORWAY IN WWII, NAZI SOLDIERS, LATER LIFE

I've just finished the first part of my taped memoirs that covered school, childhood, the moving to *Bjorkmok* (school, or neighborhood), family, and some of the children's adventures we had. After completing the school *examen* in 1924, after a time asa private tutor, I started medical school in Lund, and got on the list for studies. We were two girls among fifty male students, and started the medical list studies, after the med-can exams were over, they were over. After World War I in 1918, in 1921, women got the right to vote in Sweden. That spirit of empowerment was still prevailing (recent, fresh) in the late 1920's.

NOTE: Clearly Farmor is alluding to hear trailblazing as the first women to obtain medical degrees in Sweden to being a natural furtherance of success with suffrage and equal rights for woman, even if she is not articulating, or connecting the two explicitly. By speaking of the "spirit" of the woman's vote continuing for a decade that has to be what she means in the context of her challenges getting a medical degree.

I want to tell a story that doesn't fit into the whole pattern of the others, because it originates in my father's times, it emanates from before my time, from my father's early years of the eye clinic, when he was a bachelor, or newly married.

It turns around the doggies of course, he was always dog crazy, and we always had three dogs, one big alt terrier, or newfoundland, and two dachshunds, and they were a pattern, and interbred, etc. Not that I should tell the story, except about August. My Daddy had two dachshunds named Fitz and August, and he had them leashed so they could run behind his bicycle, and he was bicycling to his home from his clinic, one dachshund along either side of him as they were trained to run.

My mother tells how one day she slowly walked along the street to the clinic, and saw a view she would never forget. Outside the clinic stood an old-fashioned policeman, a long dark coat and a *Pickelhaube*– an old Prussian-military-style spiked gold on leather uniform hat. The policeman had pushed it back on his forehead, and was scratching his head. Looking downstairs at Fitz who was sitting in the gutter scratching his eyes with his left back rear paw.

And into the gutter rolled a porcelain eye. Fitz was a great fighter, and had fought and lost an eye. If it were an ordinary dog and an ordinary owner, Fitz would then have been put down, and replaced. But Dr. Holmström put a porcelain eye in the socket, and if it fell out, he just got another eye, as there were hundreds of porcelain eyes in the clinics. But the policeman had not seen such a thing before, and could not understand what was going on, or what was the matter, with the eye rolling in the gutter... My mother said the scene was indescribable and very funny.

There are many dog stories from similar times. Really the *bourgeoise*(middle class) of Malmö had some doggies which were really loved by the children and families, and if something happened, and if it was injured, they went to Dr. Holmström to get fixed up. Whether my father ever took payment for the pet treatment, I imagine not. But he put dogs to sleep, the big ones, were put to sleep and lying on the table, and put away just like human beings.

We return to the medical education. To the corner where we few female students sat every second or third night, where we sat during studies at Lund. I was a single woman and there were five or six boys there who were my best comrades. We had the Swedish dish called *pyt-i-panna*, kind of a mix mash of meat, potatoes, onions like corned beef hash meaning pieces in a pan).

That continued until I decided to marry in 1932, I think it was. Just before the Kreuger crash, as I remember, we [she must mean she and Åke, who were by then married] were living in the first apartment when I heard from the other upper floor through the radio telling the Krueger had shot itself.

NOTE: She is referring to Ivar Kreuger, a kind of Rockefeller of Sweden, owner of dozens of huge conglomerates with fancy stock and funding mechanisms, one of them International Match Corporation, also telecoms, etc. He died 12 March, 1932.

We had no money to buy any Kreuger papers, so we didn't lose anything, but most elder people older than us, who should have already been established, would have lost a lot of money for a long time. Kreuger was an international banker. He was the owner of the largest match-making company in Sweden, international bank, the only one in Sweden, and when it crashed, he shot himself. We heard what happened, trickling down through the building floors.

Then I married and we were married for twenty years, and as it was not a very happy marriage, even though it was rather happy when the children were born, I am going to jump over the marriage and divorce, and not talk about it.

But I am going to talk about rebuilding Apertin, which was something quite different, because I did that almost myself. We skipped over the idiot architect that we had engaged, who was a complete idiot who did not understand anything. I took over the job and it was quite a success. Now it is a place even that tourists go out of their way to visit.

It has been sold and bought by a Norwegian shoe man. But before it was sold to a man who serves food – restaurateur. They have a restaurant in one of the buildings to the side. It is said to be nice, well situated, a good quality place, not luxury, but ordinary, which is good. The owner himself seems to be Norwegian, and lives there in the summer. That is what I know about the place.

NOTE: Eric, Alex, Felix Wiberg and Winnie Gray visited in 2015 (en route from Oslo to Wilhelm's Lundsberg Skola graduation), when it was inhabited and owned by a lovely Norwegian couple in their fifties, who are friends of Nicolette Mosko-Horn of Nassau. It has been sold since. It operates as a conference center, restaurant today, called kavaljerern, or leader, and also Apertin Herrgård, or Apertin Manor. See kavaljerenapertin.se.

I saved it. It was looking awful when we bought it in 1939, at the beginning of the war, before the Germans came through to Norway. We would never have bought something in Värmland, on the border with Norway, as no one knew that Germans would invade Norway. We tried to buy a place as far from the Germans as possible. It was an old place with a wonderful history, lots of good things behind it, but it was really a ruin. Beginning to end. It was owned by an old bachelor who we bought it from. He had done his best to ruin the whole place, that's all I can say.

It was a wooden building. Restoring it is a long story. It was just almost like its back was broken – it was broken in the middle. It was all wood, and had to be jacked up, raised. Yet it was never lifted 100%, just by some degrees, so that if you let a round stone, or something, roll down from the middle of the ceiling, it would always fall down into one special corner, as it was some centimeters lower than the other. The roof peak was never fully balanced.

Then we put in parquet floors, put in staircase to the upper floor, very modern. So that a man in Arvika made something modern in glass and iron for the garden room, which really opened up the doors and windows out to the garden side (out back). It stood out into the garden, down about half the yard down, because of reparations of the house. That turned out very well.

One part I never touched was the *Ridarshallen* (Knight hall, or royal rooms) and the guest rooms over there. Nothing to do there, the guests had to walk through the *Ridarshallen* to get to the bathroom. You could not touch a 300-year-old wooden building in any special way, you had to leave it, and let the guests make the walk, which was inconvenient.

Then we put in three bathrooms in that part (the main building): upstairs and downstairs. We put two bathrooms downstairs - one on the kitchen side, and one on the family side, and one big bathroom upstairs. That was together with the children's washing room, all in the same kind of area, so that we had to walk there. There was no possibility, with such an old building, to make it more convenient for the guests, with running water for the guests.

I don't intend to tell about the stories of the divorce and all the trouble about that, when I took up my job again. I was very happy that I had my degree. I had taken up the paper. In an interval of twenty years, since I had worked with medicine. But I did take it up and started again. And I'm not going to say anything about the divorce, but Anders and Jan went to Lundsberg school, and Ann stayed with me in Karlavägen, and went to school.

We were quite happy, it was in any way happier than an unhappy marriage, which is about the worst hell you can survive.

Now I tell a story from the war period at Apertin. We really bought it in order to get as far as possible from the Germans. It was the last thing in the world to think the Germans would invade Norway. We bought Apertin as a refuge from the Germans. Then we happened to go to the nearest province – Värmland – to Norway! [Laughs].

There was nothing to do about it, we had started rebuilding the house already, so we just hoped that they would never invade Sweden. We bought it in 1939, but they did not invade Norway till April, 1940. And we had just passed a peace with Finland [the Moscow Peace

Treaty was signed on 13 March, 1940] – since the Russians had invaded Finland [30 November, 1939].

So, I took it very easy and took along a young girl, Nina Levine, her father was owner of Malmö Strumpfabrik, and we travelled to ski, up in Tretten, central Norway. On the way, we passed Oslo and stayed overnight. And I remember there were a lot of Germans in the dining room, talking loudly, bragging, behaving as they did at the time, and I was irritated, and complained of them to the concierge. My neighbor he was a German, and he bathed three times in the night, and it kept me awake. The potter's only reaction was that "did he really bathe three times in the night?" [Laugh]. No other reaction did he show. That was that.

NOTE: Since the Germans knew that their countrymen would invade in a matter of hours or days, probably multiple Germans were bathing before war broke out, rather than a single man bathing multiple times. Ofcourse, Farmor and the hotel staff had no idea of impending doom.

And we then continued to our hotel in the middle of Norway, where we started skiing and had a very nice time, and made some friends with Norwegians there. It was a very good set up, with Norwegians and Swedish, and I remember there was an English, and two others, with something to do with the later invasion. Then came the morning of the 9th of April, and Nina went down to breakfast to order it. I was just pressing trousers, we went out for that, I remember but the yellow label was a little long, so I had to do it myself. Nina went to the dining room for breakfast, and as I was putting on the trouser, she returned upstairs to our room.

She said "Märta you don't have to hurry very much, because the Germans have invaded overnight."

"Nina," I said, "you may not joke about things like that, because it is much too dangerous, and it could be true."

NOTE: Nina was a bit younger than Farmor, probably by fifteen years, so their relationship would have been more like that between an aunt or older sister.

"But Märta, it *is* true, all the other guests are sitting on the luggage down in the hall, but nobody has thought to wake us up, so we are the only ones who don't know anything. And at 8 O'clock this morning the Germans have invaded Norway."

And I just gasped. And there was nothing I could do, just put on the outfit, and go down to the dining room. Because I didn't know what to do. I didn't get any shock or anything, it was just that there was nothing to do, except to down and get breakfast.

Nobody paid any attention to us two single Swedish ladies. There were lots of men, Swedes, all in a state of upheaval, and there was a Swedish military car. We thought that maybe they could have taken us with them in the military vehicle. I still remember the name of the Swedish officer who did not do so, but don't want to tell it.

Then came a very kind elderly gentleman whom we had known who came to our table. He said "I see that you are alone and don't know what to do."

I said "I don't know what we are going to do, but I would rather stay here at the hotel, and await what will happen, and see if they are really invading Norway, and if they will fight or not."

"Yes," he said, "It is not my place to give you advice, but I see you as single ladies, who cannot connect with your families in Sweden. I advise you to take the bus to the train which connects to the train which comes from Trondheim at 5 O'clock. Even if it doesn't, *try* to get there, and pack your elegant dresses and things, and close your luggage and put it in the hotel cellar, and put on sporty clothes, and take your skis and sandwiches, and go to bus and station and see what happens, and if it does not come, which is probable, then come back to the hotel, and if not then you have not missed anything."

NOTE: His idea was clearly for them to blend in and not look like rich ladies wearing mink and carrying thousands of kronor in cash, which essentially, they were.

We had plenty of time, so we agreed that his suggestion was clever, and that we would follow it. We tried by phone to connect with Sweden, without success. My husband was in Parliament and in Stockholm, and the children were in Malmö, the worst place to be. Just Ann and Anders, they were four and six years. Something like that. And that is what I did do, so we packed the luggage, and I put on the top the mink shawl that I had, on top of the luggage, and thought to myself as I closed it that I would never see it again.

After a while, we dressed and went to the station. To see if the 5 O'clock train would come or not. Then we were standing, and there came all the cars. It was the main way up to the mountains in Norway. And all of them had their little country cabins, or huts, where they went for sporting reasons, and all the cars streamed outside of the station and further on north. And they just thought that we were all crazy to go in the wrong direction, south, on the way to Oslo. And they talked about the man called Quisling – a traitor. That was later on.

And then at the station, later in the same day was the first time I heard his name. There we were, standing. And 5 O'clock, then five minutes after five came, and still no train. But after a little while, about eight to ten minutes passed five, we heard a little peep, up around the corner we looked and we saw the smoke of the locomotive. And there it quietly came, a big train puffing slowly down to the station, and stopped before our eyes, to our very great surprise. So, we just climbed aboard the train, and it went on. And all the people driving up from Oslo thought we were going in the wrong direction.

Yes, we were going towards Oslo, as that was the direction to the Swedish border, and that was the only connection there was. And we intended to stop in the town called [she thinks] - it was a very big town. And we intended to stop off there if we could and try to get straight over the country in a car, that was our intention what to do, f we could do it, and we didn't think at all it was, and then we would not know what to do.

NOTE: They must have disembarked at the junction in Hamar, most of the way from Trondheim to Oslo, which is actually many more than six miles from Sweden, in central Norway.

Then we came to Hamar – a big town beginning with an *H*– we came there, and I said to Nina Levine. "I stay here on the train, with the skis. It is the only luggage we have, with the skis, and I will keep the contact with the train. And you are to run down to the station building and see if you can get a taxi." It was just an idea, we never thought we could but anyway.

I said "You try to catch a taxi, at any price." I had a lot of money. "Whatever it cost, find a driver to take us to the border. Then, if and when you find one, you are to wink or wave to me from there, and I take the skis and luggage." That was the plan – our intention. And she went to the building, and she called the taxis, and queerly enough, then she winked to me, and she stayed there. So, as planned, I took down the skis, and went over to take the taxi.

After I had disembarked and was carrying our skis and luggage, the train went off on its way to Oslo. So, there I was at the station, walking along, to take the taxi to the border, so everything was alright. However, when I came down, Nina then left the taxi in order to help me. At that very moment, someone else, almost certainly who had been watching us carefully, swooped in and took the taxi from us. And that was the last we saw of any taxi, or any other, at the station.

So, what to do? Soon, we were in station eating sandwiches, not knowing what to do. Two little Boy Scouts aged about twelve or so, in Boy Scout uniforms, showed up and asked us: "Can we help you in any way?" and we said "Of course you can." They told us their father was the priest in the town, and that he told them to look for people at the station that they could help.

So, they did that, and they caught up with us, and helped us. And we asked them to please get us a taxi, and to inform them that the taxi driver would be very well paid. And they said "ja" in very little voices. Then they went into the town. And the train was not regularly passing through the town, so this was our great hope before the Germans arrived from Oslo.

After half an hour the two boys very proudly came back, sitting in a taxi, and they said to us: "Here is your taxi."

We offered them money and they would not take it. So, the taxi driver said to us, "Where are you going?" We told him that we needed him to take us to the Swedish border. That was about six miles. Not too far. It was just a cross on little roads, not very much used. Towards the end there were people and soldiers, and they were building barricades, I don't know – at one piece, there was barely just so much space for the taxi to pass, and I remember that I hurt my head by having it bumped into.

NOTE: The junction they disembarked in must have been Hamar, a sizeable town north of Oslo and south of both Tretten and Trondheim. The distance of six miles, however is very misleading. Dad says that is Swedish miles, which equates to about thirty-eight US or British miles. That is why it took about two to three hours. We know they joined a Swedish train in the town of Charlottenberg, which is only thirty miles or so due east of Oslo.

After some time, let us say two or three hours, something like that, we arrived in Sweden. The Norwegian taxi driver took us to the train station. The nearer we came to it, the darker and colder and silent it was. And there were lots and lots of people on the platform, and they didn't say a word. They were just whispering. That was the first time I heard the word, or the name Quisling. The conductor from Oslo spoke about it. He was Norwegian who gave secrets, a traitor, went over to the Germans. Even Swedes did that too.

NOTE: Vidkun Quisling ruled Norway under the Nazis as prime minister until April 1945. He was tried and executed in October, 1945. He is the central character in John Steinbeck's novel *The Moon is Down*, and his name has become a noun to describe someone who betrays their own.

And now we were at the station of Charlottenberg, the border station, and I remember there was a tourist who had been at the hotel. He said to us: "When something like this happens, I get so nervous, I don't know what to do and cannot do anything."

Farmor replied: "I am just the contrary, I just when something like this happens, I become like a Field Marshall, absolutely calm, so that nobody can stir me or irritate me or anything. I order myself as absolutely normal as I should do, and don't get hysterical or anything like that. That is how I react, and I am glad that I do."

Anyway, we were sitting in a coupe, and there were lots of Swedes coming from Oslo in the cabin, which was second-class. There was a man in the cabin bragging about what he had done to help the German side. He was a Swede. Everyone in the car was silent except me. I, too, got silent and paid attention. But then I asked: "What is your name please?" and I think it was Lindström. I believe he was a Swedish Nazi who had been in Oslo, collaborating.

NOTE: This may be Rickard Lindström, President of the Social Democratic Party of Sweden's Youth League from

1922-1928, later condemned by Ture Nerman as one of the "Men of 1940."

Elena Nina Levine was younger than me. She was half Jewish, as her mother was Danish and her father was Swedish Jewish. At the time, one didn't think about it, but of course there were hysterics, amongst the Jews. But of course, one did not know at the time that they killed the Jews and chased them. One didn't know it was so bad as it was later on, as it turned out to be.

So, then we came to Karlstad and we said goodbye. I went out to Apertin, and saw what they did there, and they hadn't done anything. So, I got them (the workers) going, then I went to Gothenburg on the way to Attavara, where I was heading. I had finally managed to make contact with the children, and my mother, and the two children, and my sister (Bibi), and her two children, and another family, Backman, at Attavara, which is situated at Helmstad. So that was where I was heading.

On the way, I remember I went to the bank in Gothenburg, and thought to myself –"I have a lot of Norwegian money, and it will be worthless in a day or two, and I can try to change it here. But probably they won't change them for me, since Norway has been invaded." So, I went to the bank, and took out my Norwegian money left over, about 1,000kronor, and they changed it over to normal Swedish money without any question! Grace God that I got at least that much out! Nobody knew what they were doing, or what they should do, under the circumstances.

And when you sat on the train and looked out on the sea, you saw big hordes of German ships on their way north to Norway, in the narrow straits of water (named

Öresund) between west Sweden and east Denmark, and you could not do anything, just look at them and do nothing...

We knew at least that we didn't have very much weaponry or anything like that, but ammunition and things, because we had sent everything to Finland to help them, and later on they said that each soldier in Sweden had about one shot. So, the Swedes were just damned angry – what could they do with just one shot each? They were Volk [tough country men] enough, soldiers, but what could they do? Nothing!

Pure sin to tell it, but after the war - a year or two later - the luggage from the hotel basement arrived. I opened it up, and would you believe that there on top of it sat the mink cape – it was funny. No one had even opened the suitcase in all those years. But things like that happened in all the time (seven or eight years).

NOTE: The resort is named Glomstad Gjestehus, owned by Lisbeth and Bjorn. I have emailed them thanking them 70 years later. glomstadgjestehus.no/welcome/. I am also trying to track down the Boy Scouts of Hamar, but that might be more challenging. Also, Dad says the Swedish army did not, contrary to popular opinion, compromise its ability to defend itself by giving all their equipment to Finland, just what they could spare. Åke would have known the real scenario.

And Åke was in Stockholm but he telephoned of course. He had to be in the *Riksdagen*, the Parliament House, because he had a place there, that was his place, he couldn't come to the family. If he could have come from Stockholm, he would have had to go to Malmö, where his military station, so there was nothing to do.

Attavara was excellent, as it was out in the country where there was no people, it was very lonely and far away from civilization, so for once I was glad that we had it. We did not buy it because of the war, we had had it several years before, but it was just Åke's idea for kind of a country place. The idea was not mine – for me it was lacking society. He had his own ideas, and for once I said alright.

I should not tell anything about the Åke or Apertin time, but I am going to tell other things from that time. I want to tell a story of when I took Anders and the children's nurse to the train station to look at the German train going through from Norway to Finland during the war. It was absolutely against all the rules, and we could have been dragged into the war by those actions, but the Swedes agreed to it, even if it was a bitter drink to take.

So, I took Anders and the maid up to the station to see the German train, and there it was. There were many open train wagons with horses in them, and straw, and food for the horses. The soldiers were very friendly, German speaking. They were not at all the aggressive type of German soldiers you got the impression of through the papers, but there were no officers there.

Of course, it was the officers who were the aggressive, the Hitler's people. But the ordinary soldiers were just like ordinary human beings. And there they were, and it was a long train and it was full of soldiers, and it was full of horses, and they were staying there for the purpose of watering or something at the station.

And Anders looked very thoroughly on it, and I told him to remember and to never forget this sight, because it was a historic thing. And he still remembers and he tell it as though he was me, my age, instead of a little boy of seven or six years, whatever, and that is just that. Then that train went over with the soldiers to Finland, and what I heard was that not one of them survived, they were all killed.

NOTE: Dad is very specific about this, observing that steam locomotives as well as men and horses required fresh water at intervals of so many hours. This station was only a short distance – a few miles – from Apertin, on the way from Oslo to the main Swedish line running up central Sweden as far as the Finnish border. Dad wrote that this was the "German 163rd Infantry Division Engelbrecht (named for its commander). Divisions usually have three infantry and one artillery regiments, and some battalions, such as signals, engineering, anti-tank, and a large supply section, including medical, food, ammunition, transport, etc."

Dad further explained that the Germans and Finns fought alongside each other – at least, up to a point. When the Finns reached the extent of the territory taken from them by their arch-enemy the Russians, they stopped, in a tacit signal that they were not invading the USSR, rather reclaiming Finland. However, Hitler ordered the Germans to continue taking the fight to the Russians, and, without Finns to support them, and in enemy territory they were killed or captured pretty much to the man. At this early stage in the war they were not children or Hitler Youth, rather they were men who probably had some experience in Europe, Denmark or Norway.

Farmor continues: I cannot give an idea of how long the train was, I never looked at it that way. It was a very long train, let us see if there were twenty or thirty wagons. They were open carriages for seating persons. And for luggage. There were open doors, and the men were sitting on the floor on the straw. There was nothing spectacular to look at, just the historic moment to remember, that they let through. It was a sight of shame for the Swedes, but I wanted to remember it anyway, because it is no idea to hide what happened, though it was of course forced on us by the facts and circumstances.

But we had to do it, or go to war. It was one thing or another. And we were really a side that caved, the "given in." We were not very heroic. It was the contrary to heroic, but that is a thing to remember too. Exactly the same when Gunnar Bjorke, the doctor was preaching against welcoming to Sweden the German Jews who were saved from Europe, saying that "we have enough doctors and we don't need the German Jews." It was really very, very, very wrong, and he was really not worth very much. After the war of course, he tried to make up for it by different reasons, but he could never do so. Even if he treated a Swedish king when he died some years later, and was good physician, good internist, yet was not very great as a human being.

Now another story about Apertin, about the builder. It was at last ready, and Åke Wiberg was forty years old on the 30th of March, so I remember it very well. The floor was done up, at about that time we found out that the whole reparation was just wrong, because it was a very hard winter – minus 40 degrees. The builder, he had no sense of consequences, and cause and effect and the changing seasons, so he dug up the old earth, and left it such that it came in direct contact, or touch with the old wooden floor at the site of repairs.

Then one of the water pipes broke, and it flooded over after a while, and old mildew, or mold, started to grow on the site there. I remember one day I was going through the hall, and saw something at the floor, outside of the bathroom, and bent down to pick it up. But it would not come up, and so I said to myself, "What in heaven's name? You cannot even dust away all these big dirty things here." It was sitting there on the floor, and I could not move it, it was just there.

Then came Johansen, a worker and a handyman, or servant [*bichent*] and he just looked and stared and took a breath and drew it in sharply. Then he went almost white in the face, and dashed down to the cellar. Then he looked through an opening in the cellar, and he came up and he said to me:

"The whole house is full of mildew that covers everything and I don't know how far it has grown up, but it is just death for this building" And I got so angry, really, and I gave up, and I called Åke and I said "I give up, and I am moving from Apertin, and I am never going to see this place again, and we will sell it for nothing, because we have mildew in the whole underneath.

And then Åke Wiberg really showed himself a man. He came up to Apertin, and he looked it over, and he telephoned the greatest architect they had in Karlstad. The architect came and told us, "Yes, this is exactly the same as we have in *Grevgarden* in Karlstad, a building of the same age size type of wood, they also got mildew in it. But we saved it by building it up on cement blocks. We could do it here, also, but it will be very expensive, and I cannot guarantee it will hold." So he told us.

And Åke Wiberg said "alright we have to do it, to save the building or give it up 100%." And I was just standing there and looking," and said "I don't take part in this, I don't like it, I think its hopeless." Then it started by ripping up *riashallen* [believed to mean "makeup hall," or powder room]. Up and out came the whole floor, and we numbered the pipes, and took out the spikes, and fastened them. It was a great huge job, but we did it and it took a lot of time, at least half a year. Even the workers felt sorry for us, but when it was ready, it was alright.

Then we re-built the whole cellar and half the house, and it was really being made orderly in a normal ordinary way, and we put the whole building up on cement pillars, and there it was. And the action saved the house, so it is still standing. But now and then people have to creep in and inspect the building to ensure that there is no more mildew building, because once it starts, it starts. So far it is not started yet, so that is that.

At Apertin in the 1950s there were kings moving from the northern regions and one stayed at Apertin. They had just one room for him, yet came King Gustaf-Adolf on his huge horse Blitzen. In accommodation for his visit, one of the girls working there took care of King Gustaf-Adolf (also known as Gustavus Adolphus)' linen clothing. She took it to the cellar to clean. It didn't work to send all of the linen to a shop, so she took one item home to her bathroom to very carefully hand wash it. She managed to remove a stain on the linen garment which was from mildew, or mold. Then she ironed it, and put it back in the place it should be. Then the king came home and took the item.

Two to three weeks passed by. And then she came back, and Farmor, now acting as doctor fist, employer second, thought it was a flu, or perhaps pneumonia that she had contracted. She gave her penicillin, and wrote for her to be home as sick for two weeks, not working. Then she was alright and working for two weeks, but then relapsed, exactly the same infection. Farmor treated it the same way, and though the woman resumed work, she fell sick again after about two weeks.

Farmor became suspicious and began tracing where the girl had gone, and what she had done. Farmor learned that the girl had gotten her own skirt covered in mildew in the cellar. There was apparently a bit of mildew in the cellar and she must not have known about it. It showed itself that it must have been the mildew from the king's shirt that had infected her at first, and she acquired an ordinary pneumonia. And that was a way to tackle that problem, namely to give her big dose, and let her have four to six weeks of rest, away from labor as well as the mildew.

NOTE: This story was hard to follow. Farmor was tired, sick, dying. In the background is lively conversation by three generations about the original King Gustavus Adolphus who died around 1632. We can hear the voices of some of some of her great-grandchildren – Oscar, Wilhelm, playful in high voices, and their father, Gustaf in the background.

FARMOR – PERSONAL REMINISCES AND ANECDOTES
(By Eric Wiberg)

In December of 2017, whilst concluding this booklet, I did a thirty-second Google search on Farmor. Right away popped up this from the *Tucson Daily Citizen* in Arizona, dated 12 July, 1966:

"Dr. Märta Holmström of Sweden, reporting on northern Europe, said women there rarely reach top positions. "Sometimes it is impossible for young woman doctors with small children to use their training, because of the domestic help situation," Dr. Holmström said. "We must find solutions to help the young ones in their career. It costs each country millions in waste as long as they do not make it possible for women doctors to have their children taken care of while they use their training for the general good."

Farmor had an amazing art collection and was proud of explaining how she acquired it. One summer, my brother John and I, about seventeen, wanted to go to Europe by rail. No, she said. After being pressed for weeks, she said we could only go to Scandinavia, because "south of Denmark is heroin addicts, and Arabs – and Rod Stewart!" Yet she had a world view, traveled the planet with women's medical congresses, met Cardinal Law of the Philippines and Senator Richard Nixon when he toured the camp she ran for 100,000 refugees from the Russian iron curtain in Austria in the 1950s.

Once I brought to her home a rather arrogant world traveler from Australia who had accompanied us from Italy northwards for weeks. He was constantly bragging where he had been, and whenever he asked his hostess, Farmor, whether she also had been, she replied in the affirmative. When he had left, I asked her: "Farmor – have you really been to all those places?" And she replied: "Of course not, but I wasn't going to be over-shadowed by that young loudmouth in my own home!"

Her memory went so far back that her mother and grandmother told her that Bucharest, Hungary, was the Paris of their youths – and under the Austro-Hungarian Empire, it had been. And when John and I went to Berlin she gave us instructions on how to use a secret warren of abandoned rail tracks and stations and canals off the grid to find the infamous *Gedenkstätte Plötzensee*, where Hitler had his friends and associates tortured and murdered, and which has always been, intentionally, hard to get to. Way back in 1935 she loathed Hitler so much that, the story goes, she used every medical trick in the book to prevent Anders being born until the day after that man's birthday. It worked.

When she caught arthritis quite badly, she made the doctor – her colleague – fix her fingers "just right" so that she could both smoke and hold a pen. In 1987 she visited me on the von Eckermann estates, Edeby and Ripsa, near Nyköping. Before we returned to Stockholm together, she had a chat with the hostess, my employers, Countess Ebba von Eckermann, her friend. When I was paid for two months' work, she told me that, on Farmor's direction, the cost of phone calls to Bahamas and elsewhere would be deducted from my pay. That was only fair. It was her way of instilling a sense of fair play in me that a great experience like that wasn't just about a payday.

Some last little anecdotes. When my sister was once escorted home to Farmor's sixth-story apartment (it stretched from street to courtyard) by a young Swedish gentleman who escorted her to the Debutante Cotillion in New York, we three brothers nevertheless decided to defend her Chasity. We waited till midnight for them to return, and when he leaned in for a goodnight kiss the three of us used Farmor's handy syringes to spray water on them both from high above, silently. Then we ducked into the window. Having no idea what was happening, the moment was ruined, and after several repeats he fled in terror, and Ann trundled upstairs disgruntled!

NOTE: Sorry Sten Ankarcrona, Ann's escort to the Debutante Cotillion in New York!

I returned from many long trips, and began others, at Farmor's flat – it was our European base. John and I were due back from a month of traveling Scandinavia at midnight on a certain day. We had called perhaps twice, and send maybe a postcard or two. The ferry from Finland arrived in Stockholm about 11 p.m. and we walked and took the *tunnelbana*(tunnel train, or subway) to T-Stadion, arriving about 11:55 p.m. – five minutes before our deadline! She tried to act as casual as possible, but I know that secretly she had been rather worried. After all she had permitted two teens to cover over 1,000 miles of Scandinavia with nothing but a rail pass and a few hundred dollars, getting as far as Narvik in the Polar Circle as well as the Russian frontier.

Another time, at age 23, I returned from a year-long voyage and travels around the world to her doorstep, and it was the first familiar face or setting that I had seen in all that time. I was very emotional, describing all that I had gone through excitedly. She said – "Enough! Now, you have done it. You have grown up. Nothing more to say. Get on with it, tell no one." Then she drove me to the tropical disease ward of the *Danderyds Sjukhus* hospital which she knew well.

Once, she had returned home alone from a trip late at night. She sat down to a way-too-large chunk of cold lamb, with a glass of red wine to wash it down. The wine didn't work, and the lamb became badly lodged in her wind pipe. Unable to speak via phone, she calmly ran to the street, flagged a taxi, and signaled for the driver to take her to the hospital. She lay inverted (upside down) in the bottom of the taxi gasping for life until the doctors pulled the meat out.

Farmor was a survivor. I asked her to stay with us until the year 2000, then I was going to ask her to make it to 100, in 2005. I had a sense that she was tired of reading obituaries. She once told me that all of her friends were dead. I believe she felt it was her time. Thank goodness that Mom recorded these stories. Märta Siri Holmström Wiberg lived enough lives for many of most.

In the 1980s Farmor wrote, as I recall, some playful stories about mice. She knew several renowned children's authors and other artists. In the 1990s she showed me that she was writing her memoirs. I don't know where the papers are for those memoirs, probably they are in her arthritic handwriting, and in Swedish, and in a box somewhere in Stockholm, but that is a project for another generation to consider translating. As for carrying Åke Wiberg's legacy forward, one idea is to update his books of genealogy, now over sixty years – roughly two generations – out of date.

BAHAMAS WIBERGS' MARRIAGE MATRIX
(Just for fun, of course!)

Who met?	Where met?	When met?	Where engaged?	Where married?	Where settled?	Notes:
Jane & Anders	Nassau	1966	Nassau	New York	Nassau	over 50 years, four children, twelve grandchildren....
Ann & Gustaf	Nassau	1991	Harbour Island	Nassau	Stockholm (via UK)	to 2007, Oscar, Wilhelm Axel in Sweden
John & Satu	Nassau	1998	Nassau	Finland	Nassau	to 2004, Henrik, in Nassau
James & Aoife	Nassau	2000	Nassau	Nassau	Nassau	to 2005, Åke, Saoirse in California, then Norway in 2018
Eric & Alex	Harbour Island	2002	Harbour Island	Newport	Connecticut	to 2016, Felix, in CT & NYC
John & Sofia	Nassau	1990	Nassau	Nassau	Nassau	Oliver and Isabelle in Nassau
James & Lynette	Nassau	2007	Nassau	Nassau	Nassau	Anders, Elizabeth, and a brother on the way, in Nassau
Ann & Atle	Stockholm (a first!)	2014	Harbour Island	Harbour Island (mid-2018)	Stockholm	first to marry in Harbour Island (site of three engagements). first in 50+ years to meet outside Bahamas...

Please share this bit of family history with loved ones.....

www.ingramcontent.com/pod-product-compliance
Lightning Source LLC
Chambersburg PA
CBHW030439010526
44118CB00011B/703